Kids & Drugs:
A Parent's Guide

How to Tell if Your Child Is Using Drugs and What to Do

by Orlo Otteson and John Townsend, Ph.D.,
with Tim Rumsey, M.D.

Edited by Edward R. Sammis

This book is dedicated to Susan, whose strength has never faltered.

Published by CFS Publishing Corp.
300 Mercer Street
Suite 32M
New York, NY 10003
Manufactured in U.S.A.

In-House editor: Hedy Caplan
Designed by: Allan Mogel
Front Cover Model: Suzanne Sarah Waldman
Photographed by: John Garetti

Library of Congress Cataloging in Publication Data

Otteson, Orlo.
  Kids and drugs, a parent's guide.

  Includes index.
    1. Drug abuse.   2. Children—Drug use.   3. Parent
and child. I. Townsend, John, 1939–
II. Rumsey, Timothy. III. Sammis, Edward R.
IV. Title.
RC564.087   1983   362.8'2   83–14252
ISBN 0-913095-00-1

Contents

ABOUT THE AUTHORS:

Orlo Otteson, B.A. in English literature from Luther College Decorah, Iowa, 1961, and M.A. in American Studies from the University of Minnesota in 1972, acted as academic advisor for the Minnesota State Community College System. He has also been involved in the development and administration of many youth employment projects in the Twin Cities. He was a public relations director for the city of St. Paul from 1978 to 1980.

Prior to obtaining his Ph.D. in American Studies at the University of Minnesota in 1980, **John Townsend** received a B.A. in English literature from Wayne State University in Detroit, Michigan, in 1963, and an M.A. in English Literature from the University of Pittsburgh in 1965. Mr. Townsend served as academic advisor and teacher and Scholastic Community Representative at the University of Minnesota.

Dr. Tim Rumsey is a practicing family physician who served as Medical Director at the Helping Hand Health Center from 1975 to 1981, and has served as staff physician at Sherburne House, a halfway house for chemically dependent adolescent boys. Dr. Rumsey has also acted as Physician in Attendance at the Twin Cities' Fellowship House for Chemical Dependency, staff physician at Bremer House, a halfway house for adolescent felons, and as staff physician for the Women's Advocate Shelter, a halfway house for abused families and their children. He recently co-authored A PHYSICIAN'S GUIDE TO MEDICAL SELF-CARE with Orlo Otteson.

Preface

The purpose of this book is to inform parents, and their children, about the nature of drug use—what it is, why it is so widespread, what its risks are—and to suggest some strategies for preventing it. We believe that this book presents a comprehensive, balanced view of a difficult subject. Our aim throughout has been to maintain a reasonable and realistic stance toward drug use. Readers will discover that we strongly oppose all forms of drug use by children, and that we don't consider drug use to be normal behavior for children. But we also understand that American children live in a society that uses drugs in great quantities, and that almost all children will be exposed to some form of drug use in the course of growing up. Many will experiment with potentially hazardous drugs. Our hope is that this book will provide parents with specific information that will help them deter a child who is attracted to drugs.

This book was written with the help of many authorities from the fields of drug abuse, law enforcement, child psychology, and others. We want to especially acknowledge the contributions of Dr. Phil Bandt, former Evaluation Coordinator, Chemical Dependency Program Division, Minnesota Department of Public Welfare; Judge Allen Oleisky, District Court of Minnesota (Minneapolis); Roger Svendsen, former Director of Drug-Use Prevention, Governor's Office, State of Minnesota; Sergeant Tom Skala, Narcotics Division, Minneapolis Police Department; Jeff Powers, Program Coordinator of the Adolescent Chemical Dependency Program, St. Mary's Hospital, Minneapolis; William D. Casey, Ph.D., neurobiologist; Dr. Bill Cleary, Ph.D., St. Thomas College; Ron Lingle, Director, Sherburne House; Joan Brickman, drug counselor; the staff of the Hazelden Foundation, Center City, Minnesota; the staff of the Drug Information Service Center, University of Minnesota; the staff of the Government Publications Department, University of Minnesota Libraries; and the helpful staff at the National Institute on Drug Abuse.

The Authors
Minneapolis, Minnesota
March 1983

INTRODUCTION

"WE HAVE MET THE ENEMY AND THEY IS US"   POGO

> Is my child using drugs?
> How can I tell?
> How can I prevent it?
> Why is my child using drugs?
> What kind of drugs are they?
> What do drugs do to my child?
> What will happen to my child?
> What can I do?

Many of today's parents have asked themselves these questions—and many are afraid to learn the answers. But avoiding such questions will neither make drugs go away nor prevent normally inquisitive children from being exposed to drugs.

The surge of recreational drug use that began in the 1960's has continued unabated into the 1980's. And it has reached into all corners of society. From the glamorous worlds of sports and entertainment and politics to quiet middle-class homelife, illicit drug use is an everyday phenomenon of modern American life. No longer can we dismiss drug users and drug abusers solely as degenerates or criminals or radicals. In the words of the classic comic-strip character, Pogo: "We have met the enemy and they is us."

A comparison of recent studies of drug use with those done in 1976 provides dramatic evidence of the extent of Americans' nonmedical use of drugs.[1] For example, in 1976 the *National Survey on Drug Abuse* found that 5.5 million teenagers from the ages of twelve to seventeen had tried marijuana. By 1979, this figure had risen to 7.3 million; the 1982 survey showed a welcome decline to 6.3 million. Nearly thirteen million young people in the eighteen-to-twenty-five age bracket had smoked marijuana in 1976; by 1979, close to twenty-two million had done so; in 1982, this figure was down slightly to twenty-one million. And in 1976, there were close to fifteen million citizens over the age of twenty-five who had tried marijuana at least once; by 1979, this figure had reached nearly twenty-five million and was still increasing in 1982.

In 1976, these figures added up to some thirty-four million Americans who had engaged in some kind of marijuana use; by 1979, more than fifty-four million had tried marijuana—a figure equivalent to twenty-five percent of the total United States population.

The highest proportion of marijuana users is among eighteen- to twenty-five-year-olds: the 1979 survey reported that sixty-eight percent of this group had used marijuana; in 1982, sixty-four percent. Of these, four in ten reported that they had used it one hundred or more times. Among younger users, ages twelve to seventeen, thirty-one percent reported the use of marijuana in 1979; in 1982, a slightly lower proportion, 27 percent. And marijuana use in rural areas has caught up with use in metropolitan areas. As of 1979, sixty percent of young adults ages eighteen to twenty-five in rural America had had experience with marijuana.

The use of other illicit drugs has shown a similar rise in the last few years. In 1979, fifteen million Americans reported that they had tried cocaine; and nearly thirty-five million reported that they had used prescription stimulants, tranquilizers, or sedatives—uppers and downers—for nonmedical purposes. This widespread use of stronger drugs also occurs among school-age children: nearly two out of every five high school seniors surveyed nationwide in 1980 by the National Institute on Drug Abuse acknowledged using an illicit drug *other* than marijuana. Of these same 1980 seniors, nearly one in ten smoked marijuana on a daily basis, and three in ten reported that they got drunk once a week. Daily marijuana use by high-school seniors has been declining since 1979—down to one in sixteen in 1982—a drop attributable in part to a growing recognition of the great risk of regular marijuana use.

These figures point up a problem that many of us already understand. The nonmedical use of drugs has become an integral part of the American life-style. Powerful chemical agents previously reserved for medical use, as well as other illicit drugs, are now being sought out and used by healthy individuals to enhance their social lives and to reduce tension in their personal lives.

Is your child one of these who uses drugs? Simply put, the chances are one in three that he or she uses marijuana. The chances are one in two that he or she uses alcohol and cigarettes. And there is a fair chance that he or she uses one or more of the "hard drugs"—cocaine, heroin, barbiturates, amphetamines, and hallucinogens.

The information in this book will help you and your child understand why ours has become a drug-using culture. It describes drugs and explains what they do; it provides you with the facts needed to understand the warning signs of drug use; and it will assist you in choosing some commonsense, workable strategies for dealing with and eliminating drug use in your child's life—and perhaps in your own.

Footnote

[1] Figures cited in these paragraphs are from studies commissioned by the National Institute on Drug Abuse (NIDA): *National Survey on Drug Abuse, 1976; National Survey on Drug Abuse, 1979; National Household Survey on Drug Abuse, 1982; Student Drug Use in America, 1975–1980;* and *National High School Senior Survey, 1982.*

1
DRUGS AND AMERICAN LIFE

What You Need to Know About Drug Use

In order to truly understand your child's relationship to drugs, you first need to recognize that you—and your child—are living in a society that uses drugs in astonishing quantities. American society believes wholeheartedly in the healing and pleasurable effects of drugs. To *not* take drugs is viewed as eccentric behavior by many people. From the morning vitamin pills to the evening laxatives—often with plenty of coffee, tea, cigarettes, tranquilizers, soft drinks, and alcoholic beverages in between—Americans ingest and inhale an astounding variety of drugs each day. There are pills that put you to sleep and pills that keep you awake, syrups for coughs and capsules for colds. TV viewers who suffer from headaches, acid indigestion, hay fever, or tired blood know that they need suffer no more. There's an over-the-counter remedy waiting at the local drugstore or supermarket. Relief is but a minute away. Moreover, a visit to the doctor is often considered incomplete without the writing of a prescription for a drug. To a large degree, we are conditioned to expect that there is some drug we can take to alleviate almost every problem.

The second thing to understand about your child's drug use—or potential drug use—is that we live in a world that is changing at an unprecedented rate. With such rapid social change, young people as well as many adults have lost a sense of connection with both the past and the future, a condition that leaves many with the anxious feeling that time and events are moving too fast be understood. Many adolescents launch an almost desperate search for isolated islands of tranquility where they can escape this unsettling pace. Drugs often seem to provide an answer. With such changes in beliefs and behavior patterns, parents who wish to keep up with the changes—and still communicate a set of values that makes sense to children—have a big job on their hands.

If you are over thirty-five, you may have said to yourself, "But things weren't like this when I was young!" And you're right, especially if you're referring to drugs. We have always had alcoholics among us, of course, but their behavior is familiar—and often predictable. Besides, who doesn't get a little tipsy now and then? And we have always had addicts and "dope fiends." But we have tended to associate them with members of various groups who seemed different or were regarded as outcasts.

But today drugs are so commonplace that a parent cannot ignore them. Thus, the only valid question is, "How can I best help my child cope with this aspect of growing up?"

But before attempting to answer this and other questions, let's look at where and when drug use in our society began.

2

A Brief History of Drug Use in America

Drug use in America is nothing new. Drink was so routine an embellishment of American colonial life that the Puritans called wine "the good creature of God." In fact, alcohol accompanied the *Mayflower,* and the first Thanksgiving was spiced with cups of wine made from local grapes. Later, George Washington granted his gardeners the privilege of being drunk on Christmas, Easter, and Whitsuntide. Between 1790 and 1840 Americans drank more alcoholic beverages than at any other time in our history—nearly half a pint of hard liquor per man each day. The nation's citizens were "in a certain degree seasoned," noted one astute Scotsman.

During the Civil War, morphine was administered in large quantities to relieve the pain of wounds and the distress of dysentery. Thousands of veterans carried morphine addiction into civilian life, where it was regarded as simply an unfortunate habit. Toward the latter half of the nineteenth century, opiates such as laudanum and codeine, liberally mixed with alcohol, were the basic ingredients in the patent medicines that were peddled at the local drugstore and in the pages of mail-order catalogs. Upper- and middle-class women were among the heaviest users of these tonics.

At the turn of the century, narcotics were found in every social stratum. During this period, there were no legal restrictions on the use or sale of drugs. Drugs were freely available—and inexpensive. But the Harrison Narcotics Act of 1914 made the use of narcotics illegal, except when prescribed by a physician. By that time, America had a serious drug problem.

It was the period of the 1950's, however, that set

3

the stage for the wide acceptance of drugs in contemporary society. The decade of the fifties ushered in a major pharmacological revolution. Tranquilizers were used on a large scale to treat persons with emotional disturbances. Hospitalization of mental patients decreased dramatically. New "wonder" drugs were regularly hailed. For the first time, the general public was introduced to the notion that drugs could have a beneficial effect on the mind as well as the body. This medical revolution established the idea that mind-altering drugs have a place in society. In the words of one researcher, "For the first time potent chemicals clearly labeled as drugs were being widely used by healthy people because of their social convenience."[1]

But it was during the frenetic 1960's—a period of sometimes violent conflict—that drug use began to rise dramatically. LSD and other hallucinogens came on the scene. Many young people, and more than a few adults, used marijuana and other drugs as a way of thumbing their noses at the Establishment and as part of a quest for new experiences and new values.

By the early 1970's, American soldiers sent to Southeast Asia were bringing home a wide variety of drug problems. And by the late 1970's, the phenomenon of multiple-drug use, together with new sources of more potent drugs—Colombian and Vietnamese marijuana, Bolivian cocaine, Persian heroin—had made drug smuggling enormously profitable and had changed the character of American drug use. Hippies were no longer the only drug users; businessmen, entertainers, athletes, politicians, military personnel, factory workers, secretaries, housewives, and schoolchildren also became drug users.

Today the psychedelic life-style has receded into the background. Drug use, once a symbol of political protest, has now become simply a part of our culture,

4

which promotes regular and routine use of drugs to find pleasure, achieve identity, relieve discomfort, escape boredom, and gain acceptance.

So those of you over thirty-five are right when you complain to yourselves that "We never had such a problem with drugs." And those of you under thirty-five who grew up with the drug revolution have perhaps not yet grasped the powerful effects drugs have had on our culture. In either case, the message is clear: in order to come to grips with the reality of adolescent drug use, parents of all ages have to understand that we all live in a culture that gives great emphasis to drug use—and that puts great pressure on our children to use drugs.

Putting the Facts Together

If you as a parent are frightened by the apparent epidemic of drug taking, it's certainly understandable. You can hardly read a newspaper or magazine without reading about some drug-related problem, crime, or fatality—often involving children. As Dr. Mitchell Rosenthal, a child psychiatrist and president of Phoenix House Foundation in New York City, has said, "Youthful drug abuse today is our society's most terrifying problem. There has been no time in our recent or remote history when so much of our society has been stoned or drunk so much of the time." He adds, "Children use drugs because it is the cultural expectation. Children have been given the message by older children, young adults, rock stars, sports stars, and the so-called heroes of our society that taking drugs is OK, that getting high is something people do, that there is nothing wrong with it. They see people using drugs on television and in the movies. They pick up magazines that extol the virtues of drugs and tell kids how to use them, how to grow them, how to combine them. It is more than a license; there is an open cultural invitation to use drugs."[2]

According to this view, the cultural invitation to use drugs—reinforced daily by the pressures of TV, advertising, and the other powerful influences of the popular culture—beckons the adolescent with promises of intimacy, self-knowledge, acceptance, and bliss. There's no need to struggle through the awkward and often disappointing experiences of growing up and learning to interact with other people. There's little need to master techniques for coping with personal crises or to develop skills that allow the adolescent to meet the demands of an increasingly complex world. There's an easier way, and it's readily available: take drugs.

Some Truths About Drug Use

In view of this alluring picture of drugs, a concerned parent might well ask, "What child could possibly resist such powerful and insistent pressures to use drugs? And what can I possibly do to help my child resist them?" Well, there's much you can do. Understanding some of the factors that lead a youngster to drugs is a first step. But before we consider some of the reasons why children use drugs, let's look at a few reassuring truths.

First, most children who experiment with drugs, or who even use them on some regular basis, do not develop a drug-abuse problem. Even though the percentage of users seems alarmingly high, drug-use experts estimate that only ten percent of all youths who have anything to do with drugs will become chemically dependent or will abuse drugs on a regular basis. However, it is very important to understand that parents shouldn't minimize the potential dangers of drug use, but they should understand that drug use, in the majority of cases, does *not* lead to abuse or dependency.

Second, children use drugs for reasons as varied and complex as the children themselves. Seldom can one point to a single reason. More often, several factors, conscious and unconscious, enter into the decision to experiment or continue with drug use. So drug use or abuse is in itself no evidence that parents have failed as parents. Neither does it mean that children are failures. Children whose parents love them and have set a good example can easily be caught up in the drug scene. Their friends can often exert pressure to use drugs that is strong enough to override the best parental influences. Shame, guilt, frustration, anger, and resentment are normal responses to the discovery that your child has used or is using some form of drug. However, such responses are almost never helpful to you or your child. In the following chapters, we'll give you some advice about how to prepare a constructive frame of mind and a hopeful plan of action.

Third, almost all children will at certain times experience an urge to experiment with substances, behaviors, and ideas that are not only forbidden but sometimes dangerous—just as you probably did. Children are still children. They still tease other children. They set off fireworks and guns. They smoke cigarettes, giggle over smutty magazines, go out window peeping, ring doorbells, make anonymous phone calls, shoplift, joyride, sample beer, wine, and liquor—and today, they use marijuana and other drugs. Much of this kind of behavior is part of the growing-up process, and is dropped as children mature and learn

7

about the consequences of foolish or dangerous actions.

Fourth, drug education can help, provided it is sensible and not heavy-handed. Although exposure to information about drugs does raise a child's curiosity and may lead to experimentation, on the other hand it can prevent dangerous and irresponsible drug use. Drug education is essential because if children are determined to use drugs, they may use them in a safer way. This is an important point to understand in view of the severe effects that all drugs, including marijuana, can have on the health of a young person.

Fifth, as the problems of adolescence resolve themselves, many young people sharply reduce their drug use, or stop altogether. As relationships mature, career choices become clearer, and the pursuit of a personal identity becomes less of a crisis and more of a goal-oriented task, drugs tend to play a less important role in a youngster's life. One survey of college-age hallucinogen users has noted: "Occasionally these changes were abrupt, coming with the flash of true insight; more frequently drug use gradually tapered off and subjects noted that they didn't even consciously realize they had discontined drug use."[3]

Finally, much of drug-related behavior mimics or closely resembles normal patterns of adolescent behavior. This is a reminder that drug taking is behavior. It has a rhyme and reason as does any other behavior, and it can be understood and modified just as other behavior can. Part of adolescence involves challenging parents—testing the limits. And what better way to gain attention and stir up parents than to do drugs? As obnoxious as this behavior seems, it's important to keep it in perspective. Children have been going to the dogs for thousands of years. Consider the following quotation: "Our youth today have luxury. They

8

have bad manners, contempt for authority, disrespect for older people. Children nowadays are tyrants. They contradict their parents, gobble their food, and tyrannize their teachers." Who's speaking? Neither Grandma nor Dad nor the head of the school board. It's the Greek philosopher Socrates complaining about Athenian youth in 425 B.C.

Turning a Crisis Into an Opportunity

We have made a connection between drug use and the problems of growing up in order to increase parental understanding about youthful drug abuse. To say that drug use reflects the difficulties of growing up in a complex society is not to say that drug use and abuse is inevitable or unavoidable or irremediable. Instead, it is to suggest that concerned parents can influence the degree of drug use by understanding some of its causes—and by understanding the world in which young people live.

Caring, by itself, is not enough. Parents must also understand why children use drugs. Parents can express their care by making an effort to understand drug use and by learning how to offer help—and when to offer it. Intervention that only condemns drug use is futile. The intervention that counts is the kind that addresses the problems and needs that lead a youngster to drug use, that make drugs attractive. A child's drug use can provide an opportunity to bring the family closer together in love, hope, and understanding.

Ultimately, it is the child who makes the decision about whether to drink, smoke marijuana, or use other drugs. However, you can help your child learn to say no to drugs, or at the least to make less dangerous decisions about drug use. If we look at drug abuse as

9

a process—a chain of events that occurs over time—
we begin to realize how many opportunities we have
to step in and change the direction in which our children are moving. We cannot make our children's decisions for them, but we can better learn when and
how to act in order to help them make good decisions.
And if adults can reach out to young people with both
comprehension of their problems and compassion for
their mistakes, then it may well come about that, in
Shakespeare's words, "Out of this nettle, danger, we
pluck this flower, safety."

Footnotes

[1] Oakley Ray, *Drugs, Society, and Human Behavior,* 2nd ed. (St.
Louis: Mosby, 1978), p. 4.
[2] Robert Coram and Charlene Smith-Williams, Atlanta *Constitution,* December 14, 1980, 18A, pp. 1A.
[3] Ray, p. 364.

10

2
HOW TO TELL IF YOUR CHILD IS USING DRUGS

Some of you already know your child is using drugs. You may not know the extent of the problem, but you have seen the evidence. You have detected alcohol on his or her breath; perhaps he or she has defiantly smoked pot in your presence; or you have discovered drugs or drug paraphernalia in his or her room. Maybe your child has even been suspended from school for using drugs, or arrested for drunken driving or possession of drugs. These are some of the obvious signs of drug use. The evidence can't be denied.

However, many of you probably belong to that large group of parents who suspects and fears that a child is using drugs but who lacks direct evidence. You've probably asked yourself many questions. Why is my child so moody? Why is he or she so vague about where and with whom he or she has been? Why have his or her grades dropped? Why has he given up after-school sports? Why is she so distant, so irritable, or so hostile?

Uncharacteristic behavior in a child arouses understandable concern in a parent. And in this age of widespread drug use, two of the most urgent questions are, "How can I tell if my child's unusual behavior is related to drug use?" And, if the behavior is drug-related, "How serious is it?"

The experts tell us there are few surefire ways of detecting drug use. The behavior of occasional recreational users differs little from that of nonusers. Even regular or chronic users are often highly skilled at concealing use from their parents. So, again the question, "How can I tell if my child is using drugs?"

Unfortunately, there's no proven formula for detecting drug use. However, the information in this chapter can help you understand some of the predictors of adolescent drug use and some of the obvious warning signs. If you are attuned to your child's lifestyle and behavior, you may, by understanding some of the obvious signals, notice changes that begin to paint a picture of drug involvement.

Levels of Use

In order to develop an effective strategy for dealing with your youngster's drug use or potential drug use, you first need to understand that there are various levels and patterns of use and various types of users. To say that a child is using drugs or is "on drugs" means little until you understand the extent of the involvement and the degree of need.

For example, pot smoking, for some youngsters, may fall into the range of normal adolescent activity, much as when you smoked a few cigarettes behind the garage or sneaked some liquor from the family liquor cabinet. This doesn't mean that you need to condone drug use or that you shouldn't express your concern to your child. Even the mildest form of drug use is something to be concerned about. It does mean, however, that your response to experimental or occasional use probably should differ from your response to the discovery of heavy or chronic use. A child whose normal curiosity and sense of sociability leads him or her to sample a drug or to occasionally join in with friends is a long way away from a child who is regularly abusing drugs—or is, in fact, addicted. Drug users can be grouped into four general categories:

Experimental users

All children who use drugs start out as experimental users. These users are mainly motivated by curiosity and peer pressure. They look for a setting that is relatively safe, and they tend to rely on drug-using friends to supply the substance. Junior high school students, especially boys, frequently experiment with a variety of mood-altering substances. For many of these beginning users, drugs will never play a special or regular role. With a little experimental use, curiosity is satisfied and status with peers is gained. The effects of the drug are not highly valued and not worth the risk involved. The behavior of experimental users does not differ significantly from that of nonusers.

Casual or occasional users

The majority of experimental users soon stop using drugs entirely. And the majority of those who do continue to use them do so only on a casual or occasional basis. These users associate drugs with parties and other social activities that they would attend even if there were no drugs present. Use is irregular and usually spontaneous rather than planned. Little time or effort is devoted to obtaining drugs. Most casual or occasional users do not become regular users and do not experience psychic conflict or other seriously

13

harmful consequences. The primary reason for continued occasional use is social; it is similar to the way many adults use alcohol. This kind of use can, however, establish a lifelong pattern.

Regular users

Regular users take drugs constantly to achieve or maintain a desired state. This is the kind of use that sparks the worst fears in parents, for it foreshadows dependency and involves drug misuse and abuse. The reasons for regular use are more diverse than for experimental or occasional use and more related to the personality of the user. Regular users are more attracted to the "high"—to the pharmacological action of the drug. Regular users have some need to keep using drugs, a factor that is more important than the amount used or the frequency of use. Children who use drugs regularly develop a psychological dependency. This dependency simply means that a youngster is unhappy when the drug or the opportunity to use it is unavailable, and he or she will go out of his or her way to find the drug and a place to use it. Drugs play a significant role in the daily lives of these users; still, they can with effort remain functional enough to meet minimal social and physical needs. Regular users can cut down or even quit for a few weeks and thus maintain the delusion that there is no problem.

The lines between occasional and regular use are difficult to draw precisely. Moreover, many social users fluctuate between occasional and regular use. Regular users, however, exhibit some symptoms and behaviors that distinguish them from nonusers.

Dependent and compulsive users

Only a small minority of drug users become compulsive users. Although compulsive use usually involves

14

a high frequency of use, it can cover a range of frequencies. The central factor in defining compulsive use is the degree to which it dominates the life of an individual. Compulsive users spend a major amount of time, thought, and energy in obtaining the drug, taking the drug, and discussing the effects of the drug. Compulsive users associate almost exclusively with other drug users. Many of these drug abusers are unable to distinguish between normal and intoxicated states of mind.

"But," you may be asking, "if my child *is* using drugs, which of these users is he or she? How can I tell if my child is an experimenter or a potential addict?" Unfortunately, there are no precise ways for an untrained person to determine the extent and seriousness of a child's drug use. A professional evaluation is often needed, and we'll have more to say about that in a later chapter. But there are some signals that can suggest to you the possibility of drug use—and perhaps its extent.

But before we look at them, let's take a look at what experienced drug counselors have learned about the personalities of drug users. By understanding the type of child most likely to use or abuse drugs, you will be better able to estimate the potential for drug use in your youngster or the seriousness of an existing problem.

Profile of a Drug User

Researchers have discovered a variety of traits in children that often indicate a child's susceptibility to drug use. These *predictors,* as they're called, only suggest that a child with certain attitudes and certain patterns of behavior has a greater *likelihood* of getting involved

15

with drugs. A child can possess a number of the predictors and entirely avoid the drug scene. Still, the predictors can alert parents to the possibility that a child is heading in the direction of drug use—or is already there.

The use of alcohol by a teenager is a good predictor of marijuana use. But even more interesting is the high correlation between *nonconformity* and use of marijuana as well as other drugs. By nonconformity we mean the extent to which conventional standards of behavior and morality are rejected. The results of some ninety studies of marijuana use in secondary schools showed that marijuana users, more often than nonusers, rejected religious affiliations. They held negative attitudes toward political institutions and the law and were arrested more frequently. They were social noncomformists, as well, rejecting the work ethic and participation in community activities.[1]

One five-year study of marijuana users and non-users showed that marijuana use by suburban Boston high school students could be predicted four years in advance of initial use. Students who later became marijuana users scored high on personality tests measuring rebelliousness, untrustworthiness, sociableness, and impulsiveness. They scored low on tests that measured diligence, ambition, self-reliance, and orderliness. Lower grade-point averages and cigarette use were also found to be predictors.[2]

Another four-year study of junior high school children yielded similar results. It related marijuana use to a "deviance-prone pattern." This pattern included "lower value on achievement and greater value on independence, greater social criticism, more tolerance of deviance, and less religiosity. . . , less parental control and support, greater friends' influence, and greater friends' models and approval for drug use

. . . and more deviant behavior, less church attendance, and lower school achievement. . . . The nonusers of marijuana tend to represent the opposite pattern, a pattern of relative conventionality or conformity."[3]

Other studies show that the behavior of drug abusers, prior to using drugs, resembles that of mild delinquents. The abusers tend to be sexually active at a very young age. They tend to engage in socially unacceptable acts such as fighting, truancy, and early use of cigarettes and alcohol. They often have no strong attachments to home and are generally tolerant of deviance in others, seldom voicing strong disapproval of shoplifting or truancy, for example.

So, as you can see from these research studies, a certain pattern of behavior often precedes as well as accompanies youthful drug use. Drugs are, for many youngsters, a way of expressing rebelliousness and rejection of traditional values.

Does your child exhibit these patterns of behavior? If so, you have some reason to predict drug use. And the frequency and extent to which your child expresses these behaviors can perhaps give you a clue as to how serious the problem might be. This is not to say that *every* rebellious child is using drugs. But it does say that if your child *is* displaying some of these behaviors, there is a greater *likelihood* of drug use.

Physical and Behavioral Signs of Drug Use

We repeat, drug taking is behavior. This means drug use is a form of expression, and it has an overall pattern. In the absence of direct evidence, the key to detecting drug use and assessing its seriousness lies in parents' ability to recognize trends in their child's behavior and to ask themselves what the child is saying.

There are physical symptoms that suggest possible drug use also, and these clues cannot be ignored. Red eyes, changes in facial color, sores on the nose or mouth, bad breath, excessive perspiration, chronic fatigue, proneness to infection, drowsiness, disturbed sleep, menstrual irregularities, loss or gain in appetite, sudden craving for sweets, muddled thinking, forgetfulness, confused speech—all these signals indicate possible drug use. But they all can have other origins, too, and that is why you must look at your child's behavior as well as his or her physical symptoms.

There are many behavioral cues that can indicate involvement with drugs. But before we list them, we want to say again that all behavioral symptoms of drug use can also be attributed to other more ordinary problems of adolescence. Almost all children will exhibit one or another of these behaviors from time to time. As a parent, you must judge whether your child's behavior fits the profile of the most likely adolescent drug user, or whether it falls into a "normal" range.

Now, take a few moments to think about your child's behavior. How many of the following characteristics common to drug users does he or she exhibit?

Secretiveness

Does your child make or receive strange phone calls? Is there an unwillingness to discuss his or her whereabouts? Are there vague answers concerning who his or her companions are and what they do when they are together? Has the social circle narrowed to one small group of friends? Has there been a withdrawal from normal family activities? Is there an avoidance

18

of anyone who has expressed concern about the child's behavior? Is there a pattern of chronic lying? Is there a tendency toward keeping late hours? Is there less time spent at home? Is time at home spent alone in the privacy of bedroom or basement? Does he or she burn incense, use eye drops, or take breath fresheners?

Mood swings

Is your child often argumentative and hostile when criticized? Is he or she alert and active one day, tired and subdued the next? Is there excessive nervousness, inappropriate laughter, unusual talkativeness, restlessness, or periods of brooding and listlessness? Is there difficulty in getting along with friends?

Changes in attitudes

Are there signs of lowered self-esteem? Expressions of loneliness? Does it seem as if everything you say gets a negative response? Has there been a loss of interest in long-term goals? Are there complaints about always being watched or not being taken seriously? Is there a lack of interest in the opposite sex? Has there been a decline in personal grooming and hygiene? An increased level of carelessness in general? Have you noticed a change in your child's slang? Does the subject of drugs occur more frequently in conversation? Or, conversely, is the subject of drugs met with indifference or evasion? Or does your child reject discussion about drugs altogether and vigorously deny the existence of any problem?

School problems

Have grades become poorer over a period of time and is there less concern about them? Are there behavior problems at school? Has there been truancy or chronic tardiness? Has there been a loss of interest in school activities, clubs, or sports?

Delinquency

Are prescription drugs missing from your medicine cabinet or liquor from your bar? Have money or other items of value disappeared from your home, your neighbors' homes, or the homes of your child's friends? Are there unexpected or poorly explained withdrawals from your child's savings account? Have there been checks cashed under your signature that you don't recall writing? Have there been sudden and poorly explained increases in pocket money? Are there new clothes or other items "borrowed" from vague or unknown friends? Has your child or your child's friends been in trouble with the law? Have there been suspended license violations, arrests for reckless driving, joyriding, or involvement in high-speed accidents? Arrests for vandalism or suspicion of theft? Has your child been picked up at, or bragged about narrow escapes from, rowdy parties? Have there been frequent episodes of arguments and fights with schoolmates or family members?

Again, these signs don't necessarily prove drug use. Drugs may have nothing to do with troubling changes in your youngster's behavior. A variety of adolescent disappointments and failures may be the cause. But personal problems can also lead a child to use drugs as a means of escape. If your child is exhibiting one or more of these warning signs—secrecy, mood swings, attitude changes, school problems, or delinquency—you may be fairly certain that a problem worthy of your serious attention exists.

20

Concealing Drug Use

On the other hand, your child may well be using drugs and successfully concealing their use from you. Occasional or even regular use of marijuana or inhalants doesn't necessarily show the symptoms we have been describing. Indeed, difficult though it may be to believe, even *chronic* misuse of drugs can be masked. We know of one couple who were shocked to discover that both of their children had been misusing drugs for over two years before the use was discovered. The parents' shock was heightened by the fact that the husband was a social worker specializing in the problems of children and the wife was a chemical-dependency counselor! Both had prided themselves on what they thought was an open relationship with a high degree of communication and honesty between them and their children. Their experience illustrates two points that any drug counselor will tell you: Children can be extraordinarily adept at concealing drug use, and parents can be extraordinarily blind to their children's behavior. These are the two main factors that hamper detection of adolescent drug use.

Children do keep drug use a secret. They keep it a secret because they know their parents will disapprove, and they are able to do so because they know their parents. They know when you will not be home; they know when you will be preoccupied; they know what behavior you expect from them; they know how to please you.

The inability or unwillingness of parents to acknowledge possible drug use by their children is what drug counselors call *denial,* and it is more common than you might think. Denial is an understandable response, since many parents feel that they are solely to blame for their child's drug use. But as you will learn in a later chapter, there are many other reasons for a child's drug use besides poor family relationships.

What Is the Next Step?

In summary, there are a variety of physical and behavioral clues that suggest a child's involvement with drugs. And, although a child may try very hard to conceal drug use and may be very good at it, nonetheless, it will usually signal itself, especially if the use is chronic. When you see such signals, drug use may be suspected, even though you lack positive proof. The next logical step is to have a talk with your child. You may have already attempted this with unsatisfactory results. Still, the most direct way of determining whether your child is using drugs is to ask. Naturally, some ways of asking are better than others. But before you confront your child, you must be prepared to deal with his or her response and your own emotions.

Footnotes

[1] Oakley Ray, *Drugs, Society, and Human Behavior,* 2nd ed. (St. Louis: Mosby, 1978), pp. 17–18.
[2] Ray, p. 20.
[3] Ray, p. 20.

3

HOW TO TALK TO YOUR CHILD ABOUT DRUGS

As the parent of a child in a drug-using society, you probably find yourself in one of three positions:

• Your child isn't exhibiting any *obvious* signs of drug use, but you are worried that sooner or later he or she will use drugs or that he or she already is and is concealing the fact from you. You want to know how to initiate a discussion that will help your child say no to drugs.

• Your child is exhibiting some symptoms of drug use, and you want to confront him or her with your suspicions. But you are afraid you'll say the wrong thing. You want to know how to prepare yourself for that first confrontation.

• You know your child is using drugs, and the two of you have exchanged some words on the subject, but you want to know how to more effectively discuss drugs and drug use with him or her.

Step One: Where Do You Stand?

Before you talk to your child about drugs, regardless of which of the three positions you are in, *sit down and have a conversation with yourself about drugs.*

23

What do you really think about teenage drug use? What is the role of drugs in *your* life? The answers to these two questions should form the basis for any discussions about drugs you may have with your child.

WHY YOU SHOULD SET LIMITS

You don't have to know the chemical composition or the pharmacological effect of every drug in order to effectively talk to your child about drugs. But you need to know where you stand on the subject of drug use. Your child is entitled to know what you think about it and, furthermore, *wants* to know. He or she wants to know what *your* limits are.

Children are often naive about the consequences of their actions. They will take crazy chances, not necessarily because they are especially daring (although some are), but because they lack the experience to make sound judgments.

In many cases, all that saves them from harm is the knowledge that their parents wouldn't approve of their intended behavior—that there are limits. Limits are always being tested, of course. But without parental limits, children tend to endanger themselves more often. Drugs are dangerous. And children need to know where their parents stand on such an important subject as drug use.

SURVEY YOUR OWN ATTITUDES

How do you feel about adolescent drug use? Are you completely opposed to *any* kind of drug use? Do you tolerate cigarette smoking? Do you regard wine with meals as acceptable? Do you privately consider marijuana smoking to be a relatively harmless, even normal, form of teenage behavior? Do you reluctantly approve of underage beer drinking at weekend parties?

As you think about these questions, you may discover the answers depend largely on the role such drugs play in your own life. Perhaps you are saying, "Well, I don't take *drugs*. At least, I don't take *hard* drugs." Maybe you don't shoot heroin or snort cocaine, but if you smoke cigarettes or drink alcohol, you are using two of the most potentially addictive and deadly of drugs. So you need to take a hard look at your own attitude toward drugs and your own drug use before you speak to your children about theirs. And you need to consider all kinds of drugs.

PRESCRIPTION AND NONPRESCRIPTION DRUGS

Do you make excessive use of over-the-counter drugs? At the first sign of a cold, cough, or headache, of tension, indigestion, or constipation, do you seek relief for yourself or your child with a nonprescription medication?

How much do you depend on prescription drugs? Have you ever pressured your doctor to write a prescription that he or she really didn't think was needed? Or, does your doctor dispense prescriptions too readily? Do you use sleeping pills, tranquilizers, or sedatives? Do you take stimulants for depression or to lose weight? What do you think of people who do? Have you ever talked to your children about what to believe in TV drug commercials?

DO YOU DRINK OR SMOKE?

What are your drinking habits? What do you call a "normal" amount of alcohol per day? One drink per

25

day? More than one? Do you get drunk when you drink? Have you thought about when and why you drink? Do you have wine at meals or only on special occasions? Do you drink only on weekends or only at parties? Do you drive when you drink? Do you know what percentage of blood alcohol content (BAC) defines you as a legally drunk driver in your state? Do you permit or encourage your children to sample your drink? What kind of attitude do you communicate to your children about public drunkenness, or about portrayals of drunks in movies or on TV?

Do you or any other family member smoke? Do you think of tobacco as a drug? If you smoke, why do you? What pleasure, or relief—or grief—does smoking provide you?

HOW SELF-QUESTIONING CAN HELP

Although you may not have considered yourself a drug user, your answers to these questions can help you reach an important conclusion: All of us, adults and children, need to evaluate the role of alcohol and other chemical comforters in our lives. Do you differentiate between an adult's use of drugs and a child's use? Why is it different? What do you mean by "moderation" or "good sense?" How does one learn these qualities? In what ways do you think drugs interfere with the growing-up process? Do they actually help?

By clarifying your own attitudes toward drugs of all kinds before talking to your child, you will accomplish two important things. First, you will better understand where you stand concerning adolescent drug use. Second, you will find it easier to share with your child your observations—or puzzlements or reflections—about the use of drugs in the family and within adult society. By knowing where you stand, and by demonstrating that you have, indeed, thought about the subject, you will not only find it easier to initiate a conversation about drugs, but you will communicate to your child that you intend to take an honest approach to the subject. You are not simply going to make a threatening accusation.

Most children welcome a conversation at an adult level. Right or wrong, they all have an opinion about drug use. If you or someone else in your family smokes or drinks too much, or overuses pills, you may be sure that a child has an opinion about it. Indeed, a conversation about drugs may lead you to set drug-free goals for yourself as well as your child.

PARENTS WITH PROBLEMS

At this point, we would like to make an observation about "problem parents." Many children who abuse drugs have at least one parent with an alcohol or other chemical-dependency problem. If you or your spouse have such a problem, you already have two strikes against you as you attempt to talk to your child about possible drug use.

First, a parent with a drinking problem who warns a child about the dangers of drug use can hardly appear other than hypocritical. Second, chemically dependent parents foster a phenomenon called *enabling behavior.* Enabling behavior helps support the chemically dependent person's drug habits by avoiding mention of the problem, by overlooking the evidence of it, by accepting excuses for drug-induced behavior, by covering up for embarrassing or irresponsible behavior, and, worse, by sympathizing with the pain and difficulties the chemically dependent person creates

27

for himself or herself. Often the long-suffering spouse is "addicted" to enabling behavior—subconsciously dependent upon playing the role of a supportive martyr.

When a child of a chemically dependent parent becomes involved with drugs, the evidence is often ignored—and for a good reason. Recognition of a child's drug problem often forces parents to face their own. But not always. If you are a parent who is dealing with a drug problem of your own, you may be reluctant to take on another problem, especially one that involves your child's drug use. You may occasionally complain about it and then hope the problem will go away. But drug problems very seldom just go away. You must face your child's drug use. And you must also face up to your own. In so doing, you may turn crisis into opportunity. You may provide an opportunity for the entire family to deal with the problems created by drugs. The alternative may literally be deadly. Discovering your child dead from an overdose or a contaminated street drug is too large a price to pay for an uneasy silence.

Step Two: Getting Ready to Talk to Your Child

If you talk to your child before a crisis occurs, you have a much better chance of learning his or her views about drug use. And you may be surprised at your child's insights. Remember, most children are much closer to the problem than you are.

But, like many parents, you may have found that communication with your children, particularly if they are adolescents, has become frustrating and difficult.

28

As Dr. Hiam Ginott, a noted child psychologist, observes:

> Many teenagers have an inner radar that detects what irritates their parents. If we value neatness, our teenager will be sloppy, his room messy, his clothes repulsive, and his hair unkempt and long. If we insist on good manners, he will interrupt conversations, use profanity, and belch in company. If we enjoy language that has grace and nuance, he will speak slang. If we treasure peace, he will quarrel with our neighbors, tease their dogs, and bully their children. If we like good literature, he will fill our home with comic books. If we stress physical vigor, he will refuse to exercise. If we are concerned about health, he will wear summer clothes in freezing weather. If we are worried about air pollution and lung cancer, he will smoke like a chimney. If we prize good marks and academic standards, he will sink to the bottom of his class.[1]

During adolescent years, children go through the perfectly normal process of attempting to break away from their parents and to establish their own sense of independence and identity. In doing so, they are often reluctant to discuss freely some subjects with their parents, just as we adults don't share all our thoughts with others. Teenagers can at times be surly and withdrawn, boisterous and irresponsible, and just plain contrary. And many parents feel they don't have the time or energy to cope with such behavior.

One unfortunate result is that parents and children develop a habit of not talking to each other about feelings or ideas. Instead, conversations tend to be about *things* and *events*: clothes and dates, cars and TV shows, or household chores. In fact, one study has shown that average American parents spend only fourteen and a half minutes of each day conversing with their teenage children. And of that brief time, twelve and a half mintues are spent in organizing chores, planning schedules, or solving day-to-day problems. The remaining two minutes are hardly adequate for listening to the thoughts and feelings, the joys and disappointments, and all the interesting and sometimes frightening experiences that make up a young life. Too often, parents and children who have had little practice in discussing their feelings begin an exchange with a complaint about each other, and the conversation ends in argument and hurt feelings.

SETTING GROUND RULES

So, if you want to talk to your child about drugs, whether you suspect use or not, here are some basic ground rules:

Get a second opinion

Before you approach your child, consult your spouse or, if you are single, a trusted friend or relative who knows the child. This gives you an opportunity to express your fears or allay your anger, and will help you stay calm when you talk with your child. It helps focus the family's attention on the process of communicating. It also provides an opportunity to rehearse what it is you want to say, and to make certain that you and your spouse have an agreed-upon stand on the subject of adolescent drug use.

Use your ears first

Remind yourself to *listen*. A child will often come up with his or her own solution to a problem if you just listen quietly, occasionally acknowledging that you are listening. A parent who does most of the talking, who tells a child how he or she should feel or what he or she should say or think, only encourages resentment and passive dependence. You may be surprised at the results you can get by simply rephrasing the child's statements, and not evaluating them or offering your advice or opinion initially. Your goal is to *understand* the child's feelings. By stating his or her feelings in your words, you are letting him or her know that you are really listening. This doesn't mean that you can't "lay down the law," but a parent who does so without listening first will find himself or herself in an exasperating conflict and one that reduces the chances of helping the child develop the necessary responsibility and judgment needed to say no to drugs. (For those of you who wish to develop some active listening skills, we recommend Dr. Thomas Gordon's book, *Parent Effectiveness Training.*)

What not to do

Try to avoid these common reactions:

• *Panic.* If you discover evidence of drug use, remind yourself that most normally curious children experiment with drugs at one time or another. Be prepared to face a problem more serious than experimentation or occasional use, but until you know the extent of your child's drug use, give him or her the benefit of the doubt.

• *Anger.* Anger can have an appropriate place in a discussion, and you are entitled to express all of your feelings, including anger. But anger usually doesn't contribute much to the resolution of a problem. Ask yourself why you are angry. Dr. Gordon suggests that parents often act angrily in order to teach a child a lesson.

The way in which you express your anger can make a difference. Anger can be expressed in two general ways. To say, "I am angry," is to make a statement about how you feel and not a judgment about the child, and the reasons for the feeling can then be discussed. To say, "*You* make me angry," is an accusation that leads to guilt and resentment, and often closes off discussion.

Try to work out your anger before talking to your child. As you talk over the problem with your spouse or friend, talk about your anger. And when you talk with your child, make a conscious effort to express yourself in terms that explain *how* you feel ("I am angry") and not in terms of who you think is responsible ("You make me angry"). In emotion-laden discussions, "I am" works better than "You are."

• *Self-blame.* As we noted earlier, children are drawn to drug use for many reasons. Children of the most conscientious and loving parents sometimes turn to drugs. Many parents are afraid to face their child's drug use because they fear, often unconsciously, that the discovery will prove them to be inadequate parents, that they have somehow caused their children to use drugs. Many of these parents become *enablers.* They accept and encourage the child's excuses and rationalizations for drug use, and they even encourage the placing of responsibility elsewhere—on friends, pushers, or school pressures. Remember, although you may have failings as a parent (and who doesn't?), it is the child, *not* you, who decides to use drugs.

• *Negative messages.* Be fair. Avoid sarcasm and belittling accusations. Don't make assumptions before the facts are in. Don't load the child down with guilt and blame. Try to talk about the problem in factual, positive terms that will help both of you find a solution. After all, your final goal is to help the child become capable of making mature decisions, of overcoming mistakes by trying again, and, most important, of accepting his or her failings.

SHOULD YOU SEARCH A CHILD'S ROOM?

Many parents feel uncomfortable about searching a child's room without the child's permission. Some consider it highly distasteful, even unethical, to go through a child's drawers and pockets and closets. For others, the suspicions and fears of drug use are so strong they cannot resist. Indeed, some simply consider it their responsibility to ensure that a child is not hiding drugs in his room.

If you do decide to search the room, be prepared to handle two circumstances. First, you may discover drugs in the room—a bag of marijuana, or some substance or pill you can't identify—and, second, you should have a plan for dealing with it.

If you do turn up a drug, your immediate impulse may be to leave it and, for the moment at least, avoid the problem altogether. But this is evasion, and, as we said earlier, a parent needs to face directly the problem of drug use. If you leave it and decide to confront the youngster later, you are, in effect, telling him or her that you were unable to immediately deal with the problem in a straightforward way. And this way of dealing with difficulty does not set a good example.

Remove the drug from the child's room. You may wish to hold it until you have talked to your spouse or until you have discussed the matter with your child, or you may wish to dispose of it immediately. Possession of an illicit drug is illegal. But disposing of it is not illegal. You are not obliged to tolerate the drug's presence in your home. Some parents choose to have the substance analyzed by the police, or by a hospital if they are reluctant to approach the police, to determine its nature.

Next, tell your child that you have found drugs

in his or her room and that you have thrown them away or that you have them in safekeeping. Use the most calm, nonjudgmental language you can. You may be sick with fear and shame and anger, but be careful about the way you show it. Again, you are entitled to be angry and to express it, but you will probably regret it if you start accusing. "I am upset that this has happened," communicates a far different message than, "Why have you done this to me?" The first statement clearly communicates your feeling in a nonaccusing way. The second accuses the child of trying to "get you," which may be the last thing the child has in mind.

You may wish to tell the child that you regard drug use as a serious problem that must be discussed, but that you don't wish to discuss it right away. Give your child and yourself some time to adjust to the discovery. Tell him or her that you expect to talk about the problem later—after dinner, perhaps, or after your spouse comes home, or the next day.

THE PRIVACY ISSUE

The child's response may be an angry one. Children *do* have a right to some privacy. But they do not have a right to keep drugs in your house.

Drugs are dangerous and illegal. And you have the right and the responsibility to ensure that they stay out of your home. A search of your child's room *is* a violation of privacy, but drug use is worse. Although it is important that you acknowledge your child's anger, do not be sidetracked into an argument. Stick to the issue.

Many parents who suspect drug use and are determined to get to the bottom of it are nonetheless unwilling to search a child's room without his or her knowledge for fear of destroying mutual trust. If you are such a parent, we recommend a simple approach: Simply ask the child to go through the room *with* you.

Step Three: Talking—and Listening—to Your Child

You are now ready to have a conversation with your child about drugs. You have some basic information about them; you have examined your own use of them; and you have determined your position concerning adolescent use. You are also now acquainted with some of the basic dos and don'ts of good communication.

During the first conversation, you may have the good fortune to learn that your child has never tried drugs. You may also have a lively discussion, and you may be amazed to discover how much your child knows about drugs—and also how much misinformation he or she has. You may learn how much pressure he or she is under to try drugs. And you may learn that a firm declaration on your part such as, "I don't like drugs, and I don't want you to use them," is just the reassurance a nonuser needs to be able to say no. Such a statement may also serve to convince an experimenter that he or she doesn't really wish to use drugs again.

But, today, there is about an even chance that your child has had some kind of experience with drugs. You either suspect it, or you know it. You know that you *have* to talk with your child about it, and you are apprehensive. "What should I do? What should I say?"

SETTING GUIDELINES

Here are some guidelines for conducting a discussion about drugs that will apply to almost every family.

Pick the right time and place

Pick a place where you are sure you will not be interrupted. One parent we know found he could best talk to his daughter about her marijuana use while taking rides in the car. Get a baby-sitter, if necessary. And don't schedule a talk with your child just before an event that is important to either of you. Everyone's attention needs to be focused on drug use, and there should be time afterward for everyone to think about what has been said and what needs to be done.

Announce your intentions

Tell your child that you want to talk to him or her about drugs. If the subject has never been raised and you don't want to unduly alarm the child, tell him or her that you are generally concerned and that you want to discuss it. If your child's drug use is common knowledge in the home, emphasize that you intend to conduct a *discussion*—that you have no intention of delivering a lecture. If he or she has been using drugs, your child has probably been dreading this for a long time, so a calm and reasonable approach will help initiate a fruitful discussion. State clearly that you expect your child to show up and that nothing takes precedence. Set a time limit in advance. Usually thirty to sixty minutes is about all anyone can take of a discussion as emotion-laden as drug use. Setting a limit sometimes reassures a frightened or defiant child.

36

Set some ground rules

Make it clear that everyone will be allowed to finish what he or she wishes to say; that statements beginning with "You never . . ." or "You always . . ." are taboo; and that if anyone begins shouting, the meeting will be adjourned for a few mintues or until the next day.

Define your objectives

Let your child know that you regard drug use as a serious matter, but also that you know some kinds of drug use are more serious than others. Help him or her understand that you are more interested in finding out the true extent of use than in punishment. If your child is, indeed, using drugs, remind yourself that your objective is not to make him or her feel bad or to demonstrate how hurt and disappointed you are. Rather, you are interested in assessing the problem and then, together, in taking the necessary steps to end it. This kind of attitude looks to the future. It tells you and your child that what's done is done and that today *is* a new day.

Stick to the issue

The main goal of this conversation is to determine whether your child is using drugs and, if so, to what extent. A conversation about drugs can easily bog down. Questions that focus on the drugs themselves and where and how they were obtained are unhelpful when pushed too far. Children with a sophisticated understanding of the effects of drugs can frustrate and confuse less knowledgeable parents who try to talk about such subjects as drug chemistry or chromosome damage. In addition, most children are highly reluctant to talk about friends who are using or supplying

37

drugs. To press a child to implicate friends can often thwart useful discussions. If you discover that your child is not only using drugs but also selling them, you will have opportunities to deal later with that part of the problem.

Again, don't be sidetracked from the main issues. Is drug use going on? If so, how serious is it? And what can be done about it? Drug-using children almost always feel guilty about it, and they often try to evade the issue by claiming that the discovered drugs belong to a friend. Or, a child may try to divert attention to his or her anger over your invasion of his or her privacy. Some children will maintain that their problem is a minor one and try to distract parents with truly horrifying stories about other children. Steer away from all such discussions and stick to the issue.

Take a stand

Sometime during the meeting, explain clearly what you think about drug use. In spite of occasional protests, children *do* want guidance from their parents. They want to know what parents expect of them and what the limits are on their behavior. Even if your children don't agree with your views and reject your advice, *you* know that it is important to set standards of right conduct. Don't hesitate to do so.

Make another appointment

You will probably not exhaust the subject in one session, so establish another one. And when the first meeting has ended, *drop the subject*. If you've restricted your child's activities, make sure he or she complies. But don't nag or lecture. Don't let your child overhear you complaining about him or her to someone else, and don't compare him or her unfa-

38

vorably to brothers or sisters. Don't make your child feel worse than he or she may already feel. By setting up another meeting, you provide everyone with some relief and breathing space. Again, unless the child wants to discuss it before then, drop the subject until the next meeting.

IS YOUR CHILD FOOLING ANYONE?

Denial

Chronic drug users often resort to a psychological defense mechanism called *denial,* an often-unconscious device that causes them to reject the evidence that they have a drug problem, even though it's obvious to everyone else. They will go to absurd lengths to rationalize their behavior, and they sincerely believe many of their rationalizations. They are often extremely reluctant to admit that they cannot control their drug use, and denial is a way of covering up (in their minds only) some unpleasant truths about their behavior.

Experienced drug counselors can usually spot denial, but parents have more difficulty doing so, especially if they are reluctant to acknowledge their youngsters' drug use in the first place. Furthermore, parents don't wish to prejudge a child by assuming that there is a problem and that the child will lie about it.

And deniers can be very persuasive. Regular use of drugs almost inevitably leads to some unpleasant experiences, and chronic users will often place the blame anywhere but on their dependency on drugs.

Denial can interfere with your attempts to determine the extent and pattern of drug use. If your child is using drugs regularly, you can expect some form

39

of denial. If he or she is chemically dependent, you can count on it. If you have clear evidence of serious involvement, and your child insists that there's no problem, you also have evidence of denial, and you need outside professional assistance.

Minimizing

A child will often admit that he or she has used drugs, but then attempt to make the problem appear much less serious than it actually is.

Alibis

A child will often blame such things as school difficulties or harsh parents for his or her use of drugs. Drug use is acknowledged, but various justifications are offered to account for it. "Everybody does it" is a common alibi. Usage is not denied, but personal responsibility is.

Intellectualizing

Children sometimes try to intellectualize about drugs. They shift the conversation to theories of drug abuse, or to adult drug abuse, or to the evils of the pharmaceutical industry. This diverts attention from the child's personal drug use.

Hostility

Hostility is a common response to parental attempts to discuss drug use. Regular users often lose control over their behavior. They become angry at themselves for it and also secretly frightened. Their feelings of guilt and self-loathing are easily stirred, and anger is quickly directed at those who provoke these feelings. Becoming angry is often an effective way of halting any uncomfortable probing about one's drug use, and it also blocks the opportunity for self-examination.

40

Making a Plan

Once you have talked to your child, it is useful to sit down with your spouse or friend and try to fit the pieces together. You need to figure out the next step. If your conversation has been productive, you know what drugs your child has been using and for how long and how regularly. You have some indication of your child's attitude toward his or her drug use and drug use in general. You may have uncovered some underlying unhappiness or insecurity that needs to be addressed. Or you may have learned that your behavior is playing a role in your child's drug use. On the other hand, you may not have acquired any of this information. And you are still deeply suspicious.

What is the next step? Should you continue to go it alone, or is it time to get outside help?

Footnote

[1] Haim G. Ginott, *Between Parent and Teenager* (New York: Macmillan, 1969), p. 23.

4
WHEN AND HOW TO GET HELP

When to Get Help

The questions of when to seek professional assistance, and how and where to find it, are perplexing to many parents. Even the experts don't agree. Some advise finding help at the very first indication of drug use. Others advise first trying to solve the problem within the family. But given the uniqueness of each family, just how do you recognize when you, and your child, need help in dealing with drug use or suspected drug use?

In our view, you should seek professional assistance when your concern about drug use begins to interfere with the way you normally relate to your child and with the way the family conducts its normal activities. Concern and suspicion foster a climate of tension that creates barriers between parent and child and promotes unnecessary conflict. Parents who suspect drug use often begin to question behaviors and activities they would otherwise regard as perfectly normal. Anger and resentment as well as fears and anxieties build. Until parents alleviate their suspicions about possible drug use or determine the extent of known drug use, the tension will only increase.

You don't necessarily need proof of actual use before seeking help. If your child's behavior suggests possible drug use, and if after talking to him or her your sense of concern is not relieved, it's time to find help.

What You Can Do Until You Find Help

Sometimes the simple discovery of drug use and subsequent confrontation by parents is enough to persuade a child—especially an experimental user—to stop using drugs altogether. But for many children, this confrontation is not enough. A child who is using drugs chronically or compulsively is often out of touch with the reality of the ways in which drugs are affecting his or her life. And some children simply don't understand the hazards of drug use. If your child refuses counseling, you are *definitely* in need of some professional advice.

If you have decided to make an appointment with a professional drug counselor, it may be days before you and your child are able to obtain help. What can you do in the meantime to control your child's drug use? As we noted earlier, the easy availability of drugs is one of the main contributors to adolescent drug use. We'll talk about long-term prevention strategies later, but here are a few measures you can take immediately to reduce the opportunities for drug use until you are able to get professional help:

- Ban *any* unsupervised activities.
- Monitor all phone calls.
- Require your child to be home immediately after school.
- Prohibit any unnecessary contact with classmates or friends whom you suspect of drug use.

43

- Prohibit use of the car except when accompanied by a parent.
- Lock up the household supply of liquor, medicine, and substances that can be used as inhalants.
- Explain to the parents of your child's friends the steps you are taking and why.
- Notify your child's school counselor that your child, and possibly others, are suspected of drug use.
- Restrict your child's access to money.
- Do not leave the child at home alone.

These are drastic, short-term measures. Whether you use any or all of them will depend on your judgment of how serious your child's problem is. They are likely to produce tension, unhappiness, and hostility. But they may prompt a child to start thinking about priorities, to begin reassessing some of his or her behavior, most especially his or her drug behavior. Again, we wish to stress that these are temporary measures to be employed until you get an evaluation.

What Kind of Help to Get

Help is available. Regardless of where you live or what your circumstances are, you *can* find some kind of help. You don't have to go it alone. In the past ten years, the number of drug-treatment programs and information services has mushroomed, as has the number of people equipped to evaluate and treat a drug problem. But where do you start?

There are a number of people in your community to whom you can turn for help: your clergyman, your family doctor, your child's school counselor or school nurse, or a professional drug counselor in a private or community-sponsored drug-treatment center. Since most of us feel more comfortable talking to someone we know and trust, your clergyman or family doctor might be of help in recommending a professional capable of making a thorough evaluation. In addition, many school districts in the country now include drug counseling as part of their drug-education programs, and your child's school counselor or school nurse may be an excellent source of help.

Use the Yellow Pages in your telephone directory to find the addresses and phone numbers of drug-counseling services in your area. Look under the heading DRUG ABUSE AND ADDICTION—INFORMATION AND TREATMENT. Also check the White Pages for county and state agencies. Look for drug-treatment information listed under headings such as COMMUNITY HUMAN SERVICES, CHEMICAL DEPENDENCY, ALCOHOL AND DRUG ABUSE, HEALTH DEPARTMENT, PUBLIC HEALTH DEPARTMENT, PUBLIC WELFARE, SOCIAL SERVICES, or MENTAL HEALTH. In addition, at the end of this chapter you will find a list of public agencies that deal with drug-abuse problems. A call to your state agency will quickly put you in touch with a drug counselor who can evaluate your child's drug use.

But make sure that the professional you consult has a broad understanding of drug use and a sympathetic view of adolescent behavior in general. You have the right to expect that the evaluator you are consulting is able and willing to explore the problem with you candidly. Neither you nor your child will be helped by a person who simply denounces any kind of drug use and delivers a pat, rehearsed speech about its evils.

What Is an Evaluation?

A chemical-dependency assessment or evaluation attempts to determine a youngster's *pattern* and *degree* of drug use. If a problem exists, the counselor or evaluator will also make a recommendation for treatment. This recommendation will depend on the answers to a number of questions: How long has the child been using drugs? What kinds of drugs are being used? Is the use experimental, occasional, or regular? Or is it chronic and compulsive? Does the child only occasionally engage in reckless drug behavior, or has he lost all behavioral control?

What constitutes a good evaluation? A good evaluation will thoroughly examine three important areas.

The pattern of chemical use

The evaluator will talk to you and your child, together and separately, to try to get a picture of the child's drug use. He or she will ask you about the causes of your concern. What specific behavior in the child seems unusual? What are the signs and symptoms of drug use that you have observed? What is the pattern of use as you see it—the frequency, amount, and circumstances? Your child will be asked a number of subtle and direct questions that will probably make your child uncomfortable and may tempt him or her to lie. But a skilled, experienced professional will employ a number of techniques to get at the truth about drug use and is unlikely to be fooled by denial.

Current life

The counselor will also try to draw a picture of the child's current life. Are there special problems that could be contributing to drug use? Are they school problems? Problems with friends or with the opposite sex? Problems with parents or with brothers and sisters? And he or she may wish to talk to a child's brothers or sisters, or to others who may be able to shed light on the problem. There's nothing inappropriate about an evaluator asking other people about a child's use of drugs; however, he or she should *always* ask your permission to speak to others about your child.

Past history

A good evaluator will explore the history of the child's development. Is the child an only child, the oldest, the youngest? Has there been a death in the family, or a divorce or other major event that might have had a serious effect on the child? Are there any special learning problems? Are there any physical handicaps? Have the parents had problems with drugs? In addition, an evaluator should be capable of recognizing serious personality disorders in a child. A disturbed child may, indeed, be using drugs, but that may be minor compared to a serious psychiatric problem that requires immediate attention.

Sometimes a counselor will ask you and your child to fill out a written questionnaire or to take a test about drug use. These tools can be helpful, but they should form only one part of an evaluation. Although there are common patterns in drug use, every child is an individual, and you deserve the satisfaction of knowing that the interviewer has taken a thorough look at your child. Be sure to bring up any questions you have about the evaluation; and if you think the evaluation has been insufficient, you should consider getting a second opinion.

If the evaluation determines that your child has a drug problem, the evaluator will recommend an appropriate form of treatment or suggest several options for treatment—and their costs.

Directory of State Agencies

Alabama
Divison of Alcoholism and Drug
  Abuse
Department of Mental Health
502 Washington Avenue
Montgomery, AL 36104
(205) 834-4350

Alaska
Dept. of Health & Social
  Services
Office of Alcoholism and Drug
  Abuse
Pouch H-05-F
231 South Franklin
Juneau, AK 99811
(907) 586-6201

Arizona
Drug Abuse Section
Dept. of Health Services
Bureau of Community Services
2500 East Van Buren
Phoenix, AZ 85008
(602) 255-1238

Arkansas
Arkansas Office on Alcohol
and Drug Abuse Prevention
1515 W. 7th Avenue, Suite 300
Little Rock, AR 72202
(501) 371-2604

California
Dept. of Alcohol and Drug
  Programs
111 Capitol Mall
Suite 450
Sacramento, CA 95814
(916) 445-1940

Colorado
Alcohol and Drug Abuse
  Division
Department of Health
4210 East 11th Avenue
Denver, CO 80220
(303) 320-6137

Connecticut
Conn. Alcohol and Drug Abuse
  Council
90 Washington Street, Room 312
Hartford, CT 06115
(203) 566-4145

Delaware
Bureau of Alcoholism and Drug
  Abuse
Divison of Mental Health
1901 North Dupont Highway
Newcastle, DE 19720
(302) 421-6101

District of Columbia
D.C. Dept. of Human Resources
Mental Health, Alcohol and
  Addiction Services Branch
421 8th Street, NW
2nd Floor
Washington, DC 20004
(202) 724-5637

Florida
Drug Abuse Program
Mental Health Program Office
1317 Winewood Boulevard
Tallahassee, FL 32301
(904) 487-1842

Georgia
Alcohol and Drug Abuse Section
Div. of Mental Health & Mental
 Ret'n.
Mental Retardation
GA Dept. of Human Resources
618 Ponce De Leon Avenue,
 N.E.
Atlanta, GA 30308
(404) 894-4785

Hawaii
Department of Health
State Substance Abuse Agency
Alcohol and Drug Abuse Branch
1270 Queen Emma Street, Room
 505
Honolulu, HI 96813
(808) 548-7655

Idaho
Bureau of Substance Abuse
Department of Health & Welfare
450 West State Street, 4th Floor
Boise, ID 83720
(208) 334-4368

Illinois
Ill Dangerous Drugs Commission
300 North State Street
Suite 1500
Chicago, IL 60606
(312) 822-9860

Indiana
Division of Addiction Services
Department of Mental Health
5 Indiana Square
Indianapolis, IN 46204
(317) 232-7818

Iowa
Department of Substance Abuse
Insurance Exchange Bldg., Suite
 202
505 5th Avenue
Des Moines, IA 50319
(515) 281-3641

Kansas
Alcoholism and Drug Abuse
 Section
Dept. of Social Rehab. Service
2700 West Sixth Street
Biddle Building
Topeka, KS 66606
(913) 296-3925

Kentucky
Mental Health/Mental
 Retardation Sect
Department of Human Resources
275 East Main Street
Frankfort, KY 40621
(502) 564-2880

Louisiana
Off of Mental Health &
 Substance Abuse
Dept. of Health & Human
 Resources
655 North 5th Street
Baton Rouge, LA 70829
(504) 342-2590

Maine
Office of Alcoholism and Drug
 Abuse Prevention
Department of Human Services
32 Winthrop Street
Augusta, ME 04330
(207) 289-2781

Maryland
Maryland Drug Abuse
 Administration
201 West Preston Street
Baltimore, MD 21201
(301) 383-3959

Massachusetts
Massachusetts Dept. of Mental
 Health, Div. of Drug Rehab.
160 North Washington Street
Boston, MA 02114
(617) 727-8614

49

Michigan
Office of Substance Abuse
  Services
Department of Public Health
3500 North Logan Street
Lansing, MI 48909
(517) 373-8600

Minnesota
Chemical Dependency Program
  Division
Dept. of Public Welfare
4th Floor Centennial Building
658 Cedar Street
St. Paul, MN 55155
(612) 296-4610

Mississippi
Division of Alcohol and Drug
  Abuse
Department of Mental Health
619 Robert E. Lee State Office
  Bldg.
Jackson, MS 32901
(601) 354-7031

Missouri
Division of Alcoholism and Drug
  Abuse
Department of Mental Health
2002 Missouri Boulevard
Jefferson City, MO 65102
(314) 751-4942

Montana
Alcohol and Drug Abuse
  Division
Department of Institutions
1539 11th Avenue
Helena, MT 59601
(406) 449-2827

Nebraska
Nebraska Dept. of Public
  Institutions
Nebraska Div. on Alcoholism
  & Drug Abuse
801 West Van Dorn
Box 94728
Lincoln, NB 68509
(402) 471-2851

Nevada
Bureau of Alcohol and Drug
  Abuse
Department of Human Resources
505 East King Street
Carson City, NV 89710
(702) 885-4790

New Hampshire
Off of Alcohol & Drug Abuse
  Prevention
Health and Welfare Building
Hazen Drive
Concord, NH 03301
(603) 271-4626, 4630

New Jersey
New Jersey Division of Narcotic
  and Drug Abuse Control
129 East Hanover Street
Trenton, NJ 08605
(609) 292-8930

New Mexico
Substance Abuse Bureau
Behavioral Health Service
  Division
Health and Environment
  Department
P.O. Box 968
Santa Fe, NM 87503
(505) 827-5271 Ext. 226

50

New York
NY Off of Alcoholism and Subst
    Abuse
Divison of Substance Abuse
    Services
Executive Park South, Box 8200
Albany, NY 12203
(518) 457-4176

North Carolina
Alcohol and Drug Abuse Services
Division of MH/MR and
    Substance Abuse
325 North Salisbury Street
Albermarle Bldg., Room 1100
Raleigh, NC 27611
(919) 733-4670

North Dakota
Division of Alcoholism & Drug
    Abuse
State Department of Health
909 Basin Avenue
Bismarck, ND 58505
(701) 224-2768

Ohio
Bureau of Drug Abuse
Dept. of Mental Health and MR
65 South Front Street
Suite 211
Columbus, OH 43215
(614) 466-9023

Oklahoma
Division of Alcoholism and
Drug Abuse Programs
Department of Mental Health
4545 North Lincoln Blvd.,
    Suite 100
P.O. Box 53277
Oklahoma City, OK 73152
(405) 521-2811

Oregon
Program for Drug Problems
Oregon Mental Health Division
2575 Bittern Street, N.E.
Salem, OR 97310
(503) 378-2163

Pennsylvania
Governor's Council on Drug
    & Alcohol Abuse
2101 North Front Street
Harrisburg, PA 17120
(717) 787-9857

Rhode Island
Division of Substance Abuse
General Hospital, Building 303
Rhode Island Medical Center
Cranston, RI 02920
(401) 464-2091

South Carolina
South Carolina Commission on
    Alcohol and Drug Abuse
3700 Forest Drive
Landmark East, Suite 300
Columbia, SC 29204
(803) 758-2183

South Dakota
Division of Drugs and
    Substance Control
Department of Health
Joe Foss Building, Room 119
Pierre, SD 57501
(605) 773-3123

Tennessee
Divison of Alcohol and Drug
    Abuse
TN Dept. of Mental Health
501 Union Building
Nashville, TN 37219
(615) 741-1921

51

Texas
Drug Abuse Prevention Division
Texas Dept. of Community
 Affairs
Drug Abuse Prevention Division
210 Barton Springs Road
Austin, TX 78704
(512) 475-6351

Utah
Division of Alcoholism & Drugs
150 West North Temple,
 Suite 350
P.O. Box 2500
Salt Lake City, UT 84110
(801) 533-6532

Vermont
Alcohol and Drug Abuse
 Division
Dept. of Social and Rehab.
 Services
103 South Main Street
State Office Building
Waterbury, VT 05676
(802) 241-2170

Virginia
Division of Substance Abuse
Virginia Dept. of Mental Health
 and Mental Retardation
P.O. Box 1797
109 Governor Street
Richmond, VA 23214
(804) 786-5313

Washington
Bureau of Alcoholism &
 Substance Abuse
WA Dept. of Social & Health
 Services
Mailstop OB-44W
Olympia, WA 98504
(206) 753-3073

West Virginia
Department of Health
Alcoholism and Drug Abuse
 Program
State Capitol
1800 Kanawha Boulevard E
Charleston, WV 25305
(304) 348-3616

Wisconsin
State Bureau of Alcohol and
 Other Drug Abuse
One West Wilson Street, Room
 523
Madison, WI 53702
(608) 266-3442

Wyoming
Substance Abuse Program
Hathaway Building, 4th Floor
Cheyenne, WY 82002
(307) 777-7115

Puerto Rico
Department of Addiction
 Control Services
P.O. Box B-Y
Piedras Station, PR 00928
(809) 764-5014

American Samoa
Mental Health Clinic
Government of American Samoa
Pago Pago, AS 96799

Guam
Mental Health and Substance
 Abuse Agency
P.O. Box 20999
Guam, GU 96921
(404) 477-9704

Virgin Islands
Division of Mental Health,
  Alcoholism and Drug
  Dependency
P.O. Box 520
Christiansted
St. Croix, VI 00820
(809) 773-1192
(809) 774-4888

Trust Territories
Department of Health Services
Office of the High Commissioner
Saipan, TT 96950
(615) 741-1921

National Institute of Drug Abuse.
  *National Directory of Drug
  Abuse Treatment Programs,*
  rev. 1981.

These organizations will provide information about local agencies in your area.

5

WHAT HAPPENS TO A CHILD IN A DRUG-TREATMENT PROGRAM

Why Are Treatment Programs Necessary?

Children who have become severely chemically dependent are in a great deal of trouble. These youngsters no longer take drugs just to have fun with their friends or to be a part of the group. Rather, getting high is the way they deal with stress. But chronic drug use does not resolve the problems of growing up; it only makes them worse. Because drug use hinders the acquisition of skills and experience necessary to cope with life's difficulties, drug-dependent youngsters don't achieve normal psychological development. They don't learn how to deal with frustration, anxiety, or failure, and they don't experience the success that comes with struggle and achievement.

Ironically, without these skills, children who are chronic drug users have great difficulty giving up drugs, even when they finally recognize the damage they are doing to themselves. To insist that such children stop their drug use without help and understanding is very threatening: suddenly they must face all the pressures and problems that drugs have enabled them to avoid. To a drug-dependent child, giving up drugs not only means giving up whatever pleasures are left in drug use, it also may mean giving up the only effective way he or she has of coping with difficulties. It is a rare child who can overcome drug dependency without help.

Furthermore, parents and family very often cannot handle a child with a drug problem. Such children can be difficult—impatient, impulsive, angry, resentful, defensive, untrustworthy, and untruthful; and they are often expert at keeping the focus away from their own behavior. They try to make their parents feel they are inadequate and the cause of their drug use. They use their anger to keep parents from bringing up the subject. They mask their poor opinions of themselves with selfish behavior and an inflated sense of their own importance. In effect, they avoid looking at their own behavior and accepting responsibility for it, and instead involve their family in protecting and rescuing them from the consequences of it. They have reached a point where they are using drugs to escape the pain of self-knowledge.

For these and other reasons, parents of drug-dependent children are not well prepared to help them become drug-free. Such children often need the structured environment of a residential drug-treatment program and the help of trained drug-treatment professionals.

What Is a Treatment Program?

A good drug-treatment program provides a strongly supportive environment that helps a user weather the difficulties of giving up psychoactive substances and

55

teaches the family and the user how to maintain a drug-free life by helping them all achieve new attitudes, values, and behaviors. Users are encouraged to reconsider themselves and their relationships and attitudes to family and friends. By identifying and cultivating positive qualities, they often acquire the confidence needed to begin handling problems without the aid of drugs. In short, a successful program helps a child increase his or her sense of self-esteem and gain a greater appreciation of the responsibilities and rewards of friendship and family life.

This emphasis on personal change is the central element of a good treatment program. Until a chronic user learns new ways of thinking about himself or herself and dealing with personal problems, he or she is unlikely to become drug-free. In a treatment program, the user is helped to understand that abuse of drugs is a problem that has come to dominate his or her life. Moreover, the user sees that he or she does have the power to deal with drug dependency, and that he or she alone is responsible for dealing with it.

Why the Family Should Be Involved in Treatment

Although an unhappy family life is not the primary reason most youngsters take drugs, for many, taking drugs is a way of avoiding an unhappy family life, and frustrated family members often respond in kind by excluding the drug-using child. Furthermore, parents are sometimes confused about the stance they should take toward their child's drug use, and, therefore, they unwittingly foster it. They need help in learning to exercise authority, take positions, and set limits. In addition, many parents are simply angry about having been deceived and manipulated. They need help in dealing with feelings that can interfere with recovery. A treatment program can often alter these predicaments.

Education and behavioral change are thus as important for the other family members as they are for the drug-using child. A child in a treatment program is confronting and attempting to change feelings, attitudes, values, and relationships; and he or she is likely to become distressed, confused, and lonely as the consequences of drug dependency are faced. Parents can provide valuable help by supporting a child during his or her treatment and by actively participating in the program. Parental involvement is one of the most important elements in the entire treatment and recovery process. An adolescent drug-treatment program that fails to involve other family members is less likely to help the child come to grips with his or her problem.

The Kinds of Treatment Programs Available

There are a variety of treatment programs that help young people recover from drug dependency. They may be categorized as either *residential* (inpatient) or *nonresidential* (outpatient).

A residential program is the more intensive and structured. It is for adolescents whose problems are so severe that effective treatment requires separating them from their drug-using friends and their day-to-day activities. Most adolescent residential programs require a stay of approximately four to six weeks. Some children with more serious problems require a longer rehabilitation period—often three to six months, and sometimes up to a year.

57

Not all adolescents, however, need therapy this intensive. Many can resolve their drug problems with the help of a nonresidential program, which many treatment centers offer. Such a program allows children to live at home and to participate in the same treatment activities as inpatients. The goals of the outpatient program are identical to those of the inpatient program. In addition, adolescent drug users with less severe problems have access to and can be treated as outpatients by psychiatrists, psychologists, social workers, or drug counselors.

Few treatment programs are free. Your family health-insurance policy may cover the cost of a residential program, but few policies pay outpatient costs. Some treatment centers charge according to one's ability to pay. The subject of cost should be discussed with a counselor at the treatment center you are considering. If you can't afford it, the counselor or administrator may be able to refer you to a less expensive program.

How Does a Drug-Treatment Program Work?

To see how one successful residential program works, we visited a small, highly regarded treatment center in a midwestern city. The following description, necessarily brief, conveys a sense of the nature of the treatment process and indicates the degree of parental involvement. Different programs use different methods, but a sound program should include most of the features described here.

Most patients enter the treatment program voluntarily, but some are so ordered by a juvenile court. Those who come involuntarily are restricted to the confines of the building, but they otherwise participate in the same activities as the other resident patients.

A youngster can be assigned to either an inpatient or an outpatient program, but in either case he or she is at the center for six to seven hours during the day for counseling, education, and therapy. Children in the outpatient program usually have a more stable home environment and can respond to treatment without the total interruption of normal life required for inpatients. Children who don't respond to outpatient care can be transferred to the inpatient program.

THE FIRST DAY

Entering a treatment program can be a difficult, even dreaded, experience for a child. Many children enter with a sullen and uncooperative attitude. Many see the program as just another obstacle raised by adults, and they think they will con their way through it. Others adopt a ''stonewalling'' attitude. They refuse to discuss their problems, or they deny they have any. But despite these outwardly tough or sullen stances, many are to some extent relieved, albeit apprehensive, to be able to get help. Although they may refuse to acknowledge it, they know their drug use has been out of control and that their lives are seriously disordered. The staff at the treatment center is familiar with these and other kinds of behaviors, and they search for the right combination of toughness and compassion that will encourage a child to start helping himself or herself.

A youngster is given an introduction and orientation to the program not by an adult counselor or physician but by another adolescent who is nearing completion of the program. This senior peer explains the daily schedule, outlines the rules of the program, and informs the child about the goals of the program and how they can be reached. The senior peer is candid about the rules and about the experience of treatment, telling his or her own story of drug use to the newcomer, thereby putting into practice one of the keystones of the treatment program—peer-group support.

Within twenty-four hours, the child is given a complete physical examination to determine his or her overall health and to identify any damage drug use may have caused. Children with severe psychological problems are referred to a mental-health-care unit. Parents and siblings are often asked to complete questionnaires that provide valuable information to the counseling staff. In addition, a care plan is prepared for each child at the beginning of the program. This plan is updated as changes occur in the child and as problem areas are identified. Parents are kept informed of the child's condition and progress or lack of progress.

ESTABLISHING AN ORDERLY LIFE

The treatment program establishes a routine that not only occupies a child's time but, more important, contributes a sense of order to a life that has been badly disordered. Working on the theory that small improvements add up to big ones, residents are expected to meet the small responsibilities of housekeeping, personal hygiene, punctuality, and consideration of the feelings and rights of others. Those who have difficulty complying with the rules may find themselves the focus of counseling sessions.

The day begins with a 6:30 wake-up, followed by breakfast at 7:15 and an 8:15 room check. The balance of the day is highly structured. Mornings and afternoons are divided between periods of supervised occupational therapy sessions, peer-group counseling sessions, and classroom sessions devoted to school subjects. Although all residents are subject to the common structure, staff members respond to individual needs by providing individual counseling and other special opportunities.

At 10:30 each morning, all residents gather to learn about any changes in the daily schedule, to discuss special problems that affect the group, or to meet newcomers to the program. At 2:30 in the afternoon, they gather again for staff lectures about various aspects of chemical dependency and other drug-related topics. Following dinner, residents either visit with family members, attend support-group meetings such as Alcoholics Anonymous, or participate in community recreational activities such as dances or athletics. Youngsters having trouble complying with the rules and expectations of the program may be required to report to a "responsibility group," where they discuss their behavioral problems. These activities last until 9:00 P.M. At 9:25, staff and senior peers make a "job check" to ensure that the assigned housekeeping tasks have been performed. All residents must be in bed at 10:00, and lights go out an hour later—the end of a long, active, and structured day.

PEER-GROUP COUNSELING

Everyone in the treatment program participates twice daily in group therapy sessions. All sessions are supervised by a rehabilitation staff member who ensures that the discussions are productive and relevant. Peer-group involvement, or interaction that allows children with a common problem to help each other, is one of the most important factors in beginning and sustaining recovery.

The peer group has a unique healing power. The common problem of chemical dependency can bind members together through understanding, acceptance, and involvement in recovery. The peer group issues a tough challenge to defensive behavior, and it applies powerful pressure on an individual to change his or her behavior and outlook. It encourages youngsters to accept the reality of their drug problem and to begin taking responsibility for their own recoveries. The more experienced peer-group members understand that openness, honesty, and caring are important to recovery, and they oblige newcomers to participate in the discussions. These experienced members have heard many rationalizations for drug use, and they are not easily deceived. They are capable of getting tough with someone who is not "leveling" with himself or herself or with the group.

But the group also provides warmth and empathy in ways that a child would have difficulty finding elsewhere. This strong emotional support, the sharing and solidarity, do much to relieve a child's sense of isolation. The group's genuine care and concern help bolster a child's self-esteem when he or she begins to face the consequences of chemical dependency.

In group sessions, a child's real feelings and attitudes come out, where they can be dealt with. Often the discussions include behaviors and attitudes other than those related to drug taking. Problems with family members, friends, school, or feelings of low self-esteem, sexual attitudes, or personal values may all come under examination. Because peers understand the difficulties involved in recovery, they know how to help a demoralized member deal with his or her self-doubt, anxiety, and sense of hopelessness.

Newcomers are given hope through the firsthand descriptions of how others have struggled with their recovery problems and have overcome them. Furthermore, youngsters' sense of self-worth improves when they discover that others care enough about them to help in spite of their resistance to change. The peer group also provides youngsters with an opportunity to help others, further enhancing their sense of personal worth. Over time, with the support of the group, children discover not only that they can live without drugs but that they can find pleasure and satisfaction in a drug-free life.

OCCUPATIONAL THERAPY

Occupational therapy utilizes goal-oriented craft projects, recreational and social outings, and a social skills program to help adolescents learn to be objective, to accept responsibility, to build a strong self-image, to express feelings, and to socialize, communicate, and cooperate with others. In addition, the occupational therapy program guides adolescents toward satisfying activities that are alternatives to the drug high. With the help of these therapy sessions, residents learn to identify problems and to break down large ones into smaller, more manageable ones. Youngsters are required to set daily as well as long-range goals, and they are asked to sign a "contract" committing themselves to pursuing them.

FAMILY PARTICIPATION

In addition to the initial interviews, parents come to the treatment center twice a week for afternoon and evening sessions. The afternoon sessions consist of staff presentations about drug dependency and the recovery process. Following this, parents participate in parents-only sessions where they may freely express frustration, guilt, resentment, anger, or any other feelings created by their child's drug problem. They are urged to "get it out." They also explore new ways of communicating with their child.

After dinner, groups of ten or twelve parents meet with their children and staff members to discuss feelings and mutual problems. Everyone is encouraged to raise troublesome issues, but if important issues are being avoided, staff members often tactfully introduce subjects they think parents and children need to discuss. Although these sessions can be emotional, they are always led by a staff member who keeps them productive. Participants often feel a burden is being lifted and that a spirit of friendship and caring is growing among all the members of the family. The staff continually emphasizes that this kind of family participation is crucial to a child's recovery.

THE AFTER-CARE PROGRAM

The after-care program is another critical part of the overall recovery plan. Following the initial program, the adolescent attends after-care activities at the treatment center for a period of three months, during which time his or her progress is carefully monitored by the staff.

During the first month, youngsters return each day for four hours and participate in individual and group counseling sessions. In the second month, participation is reduced to two or three times a week—and then to once a week during the third month. Although the staff cannot force a child to participate in the after-care program, parents are informed when a child misses a session, and the child must inform the center when he is unable to attend. Supportive new friends and concerned family members, together with a new outlook and new feelings of strength and health, combine to exert strong pressure on a child to actively participate in the after-care program.

The staff regards the after-care program as central to the entire treatment process. Resuming a normal routine is difficult; the after-care period is a time for testing new skills and acquiring a new, drug-free life-style. The after-care program provides much-needed support to vulnerable children who are learning new ways of conducting their lives.

If Treatment Fails

A treatment program can give a chemically dependent child a solid start toward recovery. But continued recovery is ultimately his or her responsibility. Only the child can make the decision to use or not use drugs. If you have put your child in a drug-treatment program, you have shown a path that can help the child make better decisions and become as fine an adult as he or she is capable of becoming.

Unfortunately, many who go through treatment fail to break free of drug use. The failure rate can be very high. Treatment programs offer no guarantee that a youngster will stay drug-free.

Still, programs such as the one described are the best method yet devised for dealing with a drug problem *after* the damage has been done. What should you do if treatment fails and your child resumes using drugs? We encourage you to go back to the treatment center and discuss the available options. Sometimes a second round of inpatient care will work. Failure, though profoundly discouraging, is not the end of the line. Some parents have helped their children through treatment programs three and four times. Often, children will respond only when they are ready, and no amount of treatment can help until they reach that point.

We don't like to give up on any child, for even the most severely dependent youngster is capable of coming back; and that child, in particular, needs you. Still, sometimes parents reach the end of *their* ropes. They have taken so much time off to attend treatment sessions that they are in danger of losing their jobs; family relations are strained to the breaking point; or their own health and mental balance are suffering. And sometimes treatment centers refuse to take a patient who obstructs the progress of others, or who is recalcitrant or violent.

At such a point, you may decide you can't take any more, and you may consider drastic measures. You may insist that the child move out of the house, and you may decide to call in the police and the courts to help you. Or the child may have decided the issue by running away. But even if your child has become so ungovernable that you have given up, we can only urge you to keep the door open. Why? Here is a young woman's answer, part of a letter that appeared in Ann Landers' newspaper column:

> Shortly before my sixteenth birthday I ran away from home. I went to New York City and found a dumpy furnished room, which was all I could afford. It was infested with roaches and rats. I was afraid I would be raped by all the creepy men in the place because the door had a lousy lock that didn't work half the time. I worked nights in a bar. It was a crummy place where the only women who came in were hookers. At a time when I should have been

enjoying life and having a wonderful time, I was alone, hungry, stoned every night, and scared to death.

Five months of that life was all I could take. I swallowed my pride, called home, and asked Mom if I could come back. She said, "We'll come and get you." By that time I was an emotional wreck—messed up from uppers and downers and hooked on pot, although people say pot isn't addictive. (It was for me.) Luckily I straightened out my life, thanks to my forgiving parents and some wonderful counselors. . . .[1]

Adolescent drug dependency can be a tenacious problem and a devastating experience for many families. But there's always hope.

Footnote

[1] Minneapolis *Tribune,* December 31, 1981.

6
DRUGS AND THE LAW

Drugs and the Legal System

A child who uses drugs often gets into trouble with the law. Juvenile as well as adult drug users are picked up by the police for use, possession or sale of illegal substances, and for crimes related to drug use, such as theft, armed robbery, and burglary; mugging and other crimes of violence; prostitution; and reckless and hit-and-run driving. Judges and probation officers testify to the role drugs play in the lives of young people. One judge we interviewed estimated that up to seventy percent of the juveniles who appear before his bench are involved with drugs.

Every child who uses drugs risks arrest and legal penalties. The letter of the law makes it illegal for minors to possess, purchase, or attempt to purchase any alcoholic beverages. The same is true for tobacco products in most states. Except for legitimate medical or research purposes, it is illegal by federal or state laws for *anyone* to possess, sell, or intend to sell drugs that are defined as "controlled substances." These include marijuana, hashish, cocaine, heroin, LSD, PCP, peyote, amphetamines, barbiturates, and a variety of other prescription drugs.

68

Laws vary from state to state. In some states, the penalty for possession of a small amount of marijuana for personal use has been reduced to a misdemeanor. In practice, marijuana smoking has become so common that its use is sometimes ignored by law enforcement officers; but it is nevertheless illegal, and can quickly become a focus of police attention if there is other suspicious behavior.

Children know that drugs are illegal, but many users develop a contempt for the law and the juvenile justice system, which is often slowmoving and lenient.

This attitude is readily transmitted to younger children who want to emulate and be accepted by older children. The result is that many adolescents are genuinely surprised when they find themselves locked up in a juvenile detention center on a drug charge.

The Link Between Drugs and Crime

The traditional view has been that drug use leads to crime. Some researchers now think that delinquent behavior precedes drug use. In either case, the link between drug use and juvenile crime is unarguable: children who use drugs are in legal trouble far more often than children who don't.

Adolescents who use drugs regularly, especially those with a chemical dependency, find themselves relying mainly on drug-using friends for companionship. Their nonusing friends often refuse to tolerate their drug use and eventually stop seeing them. As a result, drug-using friends become the only social life they have, and drug use the only way to cope with the world.

This is one reason why it is very difficult for

some adolescent users to quit: they have no social activities apart from their friends. Doing drugs *is* social activity—the only time they feel comfortable and intimate and a part of something. They have not learned patience, fortitude, and faith in themselves, so they turn to drugs when there is a crisis. The younger the user, the less chance he or she has to mature, and the harder it is to give up drugs. When one has no friends or interests outside of drugs, it is frightening to think about giving them up.

Often, these associations lead a child to crime. Drugs cost money. Many youngsters begin to support their drug use by extorting money from younger children, or by stealing from family, friends, and friends' families. Cash, jewelry, TVs—anything that can be swapped or sold for drugs may be stolen.

The next step for a regular user is dealing. The process is almost always a gradual, inconspicuous transformation from sharing to selling for profit. The user with a supply first gains status by sharing it with friends. If the requests increase, friends are asked to pay their share. Then, the user decides to price their share high enough to cover the costs of his or her own. As the number who buy increases, there are fewer friends in it for whom the supplier is doing a favor, and it becomes clear that he or she deserves a profit. The user is now a dealer—and ripe for trouble.

Not only are the penalties for selling drugs far more severe than those for simple possession, but the possibility of danger and tragedy dramatically increases for a youngster who associates with dealers. Dealing is one of the most dangerous activities a child can be involved in.

Many adolescents who find comfort and excitement in heavy drug use want to become "street-wise,"

70

and they can get into serious trouble before they know it. Children who begin dealing may quickly find themselves associating with society's most violent criminals. Many experienced dealers are unstable users who would not hesitate to murder someone they suspected (often irrationally) of trying to cheat them or of informing on them.

Drugs are big business with opportunities for big profits. The international traffic is run by organized professionals who have usually been criminals all their lives. They are cold-blooded and dangerous.

What to Do if Your Child Is Arrested

Be sure your child understands the risks and penalties of drug use, and if you suspect your child is using drugs, be prepared for his or her possible arrest. What are the police and court procedures? What is likely to happen to your child? What kind of help can you get from the courts?

An arrest, "getting busted," is a frightening experience for a child and shocking to parents. The child is brought to the police station, fingerprinted, and booked just like any other lawbreaker. The way you respond can make a big difference to your child and to what happens to him or her.

Juveniles—the age limit varies from state to state—are treated differently from adults. Normally, the police will call you right away, and, unless the charge is extremely serious, they will release your child into your custody as soon as you report to the police station. A few parents are tempted to "teach the kid a lesson" by letting him or her remain in jail. But don't refuse to go. Your child needs someone, and you are still the one he or she turns to in time of trouble, even though he or she seems to be the cause of most of it.

What to Do at the Police Station

When you meet your child at the police station or jail, do two things: *stay calm* and *find out what happened.* A hysterical or angry reaction will not help your child or the situation. Don't prejudge the child or the police. Form your conclusions after you've heard both sides of the story.

Find out from the police what the police report says. And remember that the police are just doing the job you pay them to do; they aren't deliberately picking on your child. Although police sometimes do make mistakes, they very seldom arrest a child without evidence of delinquent behavior. Find out the facts as the police saw them, and *don't argue.* Then arrange for your child's release.

When you see your child, make it clear that he or she *will* be coming home with you. Don't argue; don't lecture; don't accuse him or her at the police station, and don't try to extract information about his or her friends or drug contacts.

Whether he or she is visibly upset or trying to act tough, your child is in distress, and the less said at the station, the better. Make it clear there will be time later to talk.

Should You Get a Lawyer?

Most juvenile court authorities recommend that you retain an attorney, if possible. And they suggest that you get one with experience in the juvenile courts—a qualification your family lawyer may not have. A qualified attorney can provide valuable guidance throughout the proceedings.

Attorneys' services are expensive, however. If you can't afford one, or if you can't find one with appropriate experience, consult the Legal Aid Society or the Public Defender's Office in your community.

How the Juvenile Court Can Help You and Your Child

Most juvenile courts have a philosophy of rehabilitation. Regardless of the seriousness of the charge, court authorities recognize that they are dealing with children who are capable of changing. For this reason, juvenile court records are kept confidential. A child's delinquent behavior does not become part of a record that follows him or her into adulthood. Moreover, the name of an arrested juvenile is not published in the newspapers and the charge is not publicized.

Juvenile courts are primarily interested in helping delinquent children become responsible members of society. Accordingly, they try to steer users and their families into appropriate treatment programs. Parents should approach the court in a spirit of cooperation. Parents' attitudes often affect the disposition of the court toward the child, and this influences the kind of penalty or rehabilitative program the court imposes.

A word of caution: some parents and children have a mistaken notion that a charge for a crime other than a drug violation will be dismissed or reduced if a child acknowledges a drug problem and agrees to enter a treatment program. This belief arises out of

73

the reluctance of juvenile courts to send young of-
fenders to detention homes or prisons. Many states
require up to three convictions before any jail time
can be served by juveniles, and some underage delinquents think they can take advantage of such a pro-
vision. But although the court may indeed recommend
leniency as well as a treatment program for a drug-
using juvenile, if a child has broken laws in addition
to the drug statutes, the court will take it into account,
and the child must be prepared to pay the consequences. Drug use does not excuse criminal behavior.

What Happens in Court?

Following your child's arrest and release into your
custody, the police will prepare a report and decide
whether to file charges. This can take days or even
weeks. During this time, a police officer or a juvenile
probation worker may call on you or your child to
obtain additional information.

Once in court, a child charged with a drug offense, or a crime involving drugs, goes through the
same procedure as any other juvenile offender. This
procedure may vary from court to court, but in general, there will be two hearings: an *arraignment hearing* and a *disposition hearing*.

At the arraignment hearing the charges are read,
the police report is submitted, and any other evidence
or testimony, including anything you, your child, or
your attorney might wish to say, is presented to the
presiding judge. A court-appointed investigating officer summarizes the child's special needs and problems, and makes a recommendation to the court. Although this is a formal hearing, it is often conducted
somewhat informally. Others present are asked to ex-

press their ideas about what is best for the child, and parents are given every opportunity to offer ideas and comment on the suggestions of others.

At the disposition hearing, a decision is made about what is to be done with the child. This decision may be made immediately following the arraignment hearing, or it may be delayed to allow for additional investigation of the child and the family. So that the best interests of the child may be met, careful consideration is given to the problem that brought the child into court—whether it was criminal behavior, family conflict, or drug use. If a child fails to respond to the recommended course of action, a second disposition hearing may be held, even though the child has not committed another offense.

What Happens to Your Child

A juvenile court has numerous options. What happens to your child depends on the seriousness of the drug use, the seriousness of the criminal offense, his or her attitude, and the family's attitude.

The most lenient course the judge can take is to continue, or postpone, the case, usually for ninety days, during which time a court-appointed probation officer observes the child and his or her family to see if they can manage without further court involvement. If they can, the charge is often dismissed.

For greater penalties, the judge may require the child and his or her family to attend drug and/or family counseling sessions conducted by community agencies. Or the child may be committed to a drug-treatment program.

In addition, if other than drug offenses are involved, the court may require that restitution for damages be made to a victim, or that similar payment be made to charity if the victim is unknown. The child may be placed on probation, required to obey strict rules, and report regularly to a probation officer. He or she may also be required to contribute a specified number of hours of unpaid labor to cleanup or conservation work or to community service.

More drastic measures include assignment to a state training school or juvenile detention home. If the family situation is particularly difficult, a child may be sent to a court-approved foster home.

The Law and the Family

A family that has been through an experience with the police and the courts knows how embarassing, anguishing, and exhausting it can be. But such a family may also have found some rewards. Perhaps for the first time in a long time the family has come together. In such a crisis, everything is out in the open, and there is hope for change.

One of the blessings in disguise of court involvement is that punishment is imposed on the child by a power outside of the family. No longer is it a case of the child against the parent; now there is an opportunity for the parent and the child to unite. "I'll help you get through this" can be very comforting words to a child who needs help from someone he or she can count on.

It is also a time for the child to learn what it means to take responsibility for one's actions, and to learn that people love in spite of one's mistakes—and that mistakes can be forgiven. By seeing the crisis through together, families get a chance to become

76

stronger, and children get a chance to see how difficult problems can be solved.

Thus, it is in everyone's best interests to support the child and the court. We urge you to follow the court's recommendations; they are trying very hard to deal with drug use in America. If you are unfortunate enough to have to see your child in court, we hope you will realize that the courts need help with this problem, and that it must come from you.

7
WHY CHILDREN USE DRUGS

Much has been written about the reasons children use drugs. They are pictured as bored, frustrated, rebellious, anxious about their identities, addled by too much TV, brainwashed by drug commercials, caught up in thrill seeking and escape. Although these factors undoubtedly contribute to an adolescent's decision to use drugs, there is another more important factor that is often overlooked or simply ignored. *Children take drugs because it is fun to take drugs.* If drugs weren't fun, young people wouldn't use them. "I know all the facts," says a junior at an Atlanta, Georgia, high school. "I know marijuana is fat soluble, and I know it lowers my sex hormones, but it makes you feel good. That's why kids smoke it; it makes them feel good."[1]

Pleasure is drug taking's primary attraction, but a surprising number of people seem unwilling to accept this. This unwillingness, or inability, to see the obvious is most often revealed in the anguished question, "Why do kids need to take drugs?" As Harrison Pope remarked in his useful book about the sixties's drug scene, *Voices From the Drug Culture,* "Marijuana or LSD use is very rarely the compulsive satisfaction of an acute need. Practically all users perceive taking these drugs as mere enjoyment. The user feels no more *need* to take hallucinogens than another person feels a need to drive a sports car."[2]

The drugs that are taken for pleasure—the *sensual drugs* as researcher Dr. Hardin Jones[3] calls them—*do* alter consciousness. And there are those who argue that because drug taking is a universal phenomenon, stretching back through all of recorded history and touching all cultures, there must be an innate human need to periodically alter consciousness. According to this view, drug use is the result of a normal drive, a drive similar to hunger or sex; and much historical, anthropological, psychological, and even medical evidence can be presented in support of this supposition. But whether one accepts this view or not, it seems more helpful to look at drug use the way most drug users look at it, and the vast majority of drug users look to drugs for enjoyment and excitement.

Many people find this view upsetting. To seek pleasure through drugs seems to go against the grain of the American belief in the work ethic—that a deliberate squandering of valuable time and energy in the pursuit of pleasure is wrong. Nevertheless, to deny that drug users *are* having fun is, in Pope's words, "to forfeit any chance of understanding drug use." If your child is using drugs, you must recognize that drugs' first appeal is to a sense of fun. You may well discover that there are other reasons besides pleasure-seeking underlying a youngster's habitual drug use, but it is the pleasure-producing aspects of drugs that make their attraction so powerful.

A word of reassurance. As a parent, you can help your children cope with the seductive, pleasure-producing element of drug use. You can help them see that they cannot long survive in the world if they allow pursuit of pleasurable gratification to render them vulnerable. You can help your children learn what you have learned: that life has its highs and lows; that struggle and loss are unavoidable; that everything has a price. You must help them learn how to acquire the mental skills and emotional balance that will allow them not only to survive but to find and enjoy the best in life—without drugs.

Having fun is, of course, one of the blessings of childhood. We should encourage our children to have fun. For that matter, we would like to have more of it ourselves. But as parents we should know that some kinds of fun are too dangerous for our children. And drug taking is one kind of fun that can have grave consequences. If you want to help your children develop responsible attitudes toward drugs and fun, you need to understand why, given all the other legal, safe, and readily available ways there are to have fun, many children still choose drugs. Let's take a closer look at some of the reasons other than pleasure for adolescent drug use.

Drugs and Availability

Drug experts agree that drug use is directly related to availability. And drugs *are* available. Marijuana is easy to get. Alcohol more so. And other drugs can usually be obtained with little effort. Probably every American adolescent either knows someone who is dealing or has a friend who can get drugs. Given the almost unlimited availability of drugs today, you can be virtually certain that by the age of twelve your child has been presented with ample opportunity to sample them. And they're everywhere. You can't move elsewhere in hopes of escaping them. Rural and small-town America is no longer a shelter from the big-city problem of drug use. A 1979 survey by the National Institute on Drug Abuse found that drug use in rural sections of the country has nearly reached the level of use in metropolitan areas.

In addition, because the legal penalties for possession and use have greatly diminished over the past ten years, especially for marijuana, drugs are now more available and more socially acceptable. Many expert observers of the drug scene see a direct relation between legal risk, availability, and use. The higher the legal penalties for possessing and dealing in drugs, the more difficult they are to obtain; and the more difficult they are to obtain, the less they will be used.

Drugs and Peer Pressure

A youngster's decision about whether to sample a drug is highly influenced by the degree of pressure he or she gets from peers. The sense of belonging is extremely important, especially for children. Children need to be liked, to be viewed as good sports, and to be part of the crowd. The social pressure of peers can be overwhelming. It is a rare child who will risk losing friends. Peer pressure and normal curiosity are often strong enough to override the most strenuous parental objections to drug use.

Pot smoking provides an example of how peer pressure can operate. Smoking marijuana in the company of others usually follows a prescribed etiquette. The pot itself is regarded as community property. Once lighted, the joint or pipe is passed around to everyone present, and it may make the rounds several times. A child who chooses not to smoke it usually must repeatedly decline it, and this decision can cause the other members of the group to feel uncomfortable or to even express their disapproval of the nonsmoker.

It's very difficult for nonsmokers to enjoy themselves under those circumstances. And the decision to leave the company of friends is not easy. It's little wonder that a young person, faced with a choice between uneasy participation and social ostracism, will choose to go along. As one teenage girl said about pot smoking, "You can't help but get stoned. Just everywhere you go everyone has it. It's hard to turn the thing down."[4]

Drugs and Sociability

Children are attracted by the adventure and companionship that accompany an invitation to join a circle of friends that is doing drugs. One eighteen-year-old boy recalled his initial experience with drugs this way:

> I first started smoking pot when I was in the ninth grade. I was aware that people smoked pot but I never was invited. I wasn't really concerned about it—besides the fact that I was not invited. I first smoked with a friend I had met earlier that year. He invited me over to his house after school. I didn't know he smoked until he brought out his stash. Needless to say, I was intrigued by the mystique of a substance that altered your outlook on life and made things seem less painful, and a lot more humorous. He rolled a joint and we smoked it. . . . I was thrilled to have done it. I felt a little older and wiser and very pleased with myself for being invited to "party" with someone. Up to that time I wasn't all that popular. I think somewhere along the line I started thinking that people who smoked pot were more appealing to other

people their age because of the new and totally different thing they were doing. They seemed to be freer
and happier to be around.[5]

It's clear from this boy's account that being "in-
vited to party" was more important than the actual
experience of smoking. For many youngsters, drug
use provides some immediate relief from a sense of
isolation. Using drugs is a good way to meet people.
To take drugs with someone is often the first step in
getting acquainted. Many teenagers make drug use an
absolute prerequisite for friendship. A youngster who
refuses drugs is often rejected. Joining a group of drug
users is more often than not a way of getting to know
others, especially members of the opposite sex.

Adults who judge this behavior severely need to
consider the millions of relationships begun with the
ritualized exchange of nicotine and alcohol in a bar.
As with alcohol, many drugs can make young people
feel aggressive, confident, euphoric, and talkative.
Although they seem an ideal vehicle for meeting people, drugs ultimately impair the ability to relate effectively.

Drugs as a Rite of Passage

The connection between drugs and the social behavior
of adolescents suggests that drug use today represents
something of a rite of passage into adulthood. All
societies, primitive and modern, offer adolescents
some form of initiation into adulthood. Some initia-
tions are quite formal and even severe. In western
societies, they are much less ritualized and are often
left to the family to define.

In America, graduation from high school is perhaps the most significant marker between adolescence and adulthood. But today, since we now expect so many of our children to go on to college, even this event has lost much of its psychological force. Entry into the adult world is often delayed well into one's twenties. An American childhood is thus often an extended experience, with only the loosest ties to the stable traditions of earlier generations.

But even for all the lack of a formal ritual that signals entry into adulthood, children still intuitively sense that they need such a rite. For this reason, much of what we call drug behavior can be seen as "initiation behavior." It's behavior that is secretive, ritualistic, and testing. It forms a bond among initiates. It excludes outsiders. Here are the words of one young man describing the experience of initiating novices to drugs:

> I really enjoy turning on somebody to dope for the first time. I guess it's partly a power trip thing. You know all about it and he doesn't, and it's sort of fun to teach him what it's like, to be a father to him. And there's a sense of responsibility to it, too. You want to be sure he'll have a good time, make sure he's not anxious, be careful not to try to force your ideas on him as to what you think is good about it. You just let him do his thing and get into his own head. Then you play him some good rock on a good hi-fi system, and he listens for a minute, and his eyes light up, and he looks back at you with this look of discovery on his face. Suddenly he *knows* why rock sounds this way. Suddenly he understands a whole lot of things. And that gives me a really cool feeling, to know that there's one more person who knows, one more person who's begun to see through all the programming he's gotten since he was born.[6]

84

Just as many primitive tribes use hallucinogenic drugs to initiate adolescents into adulthood, so do older guides induct many American teenagers into the rituals and seeming wisdom of the drug subculture.

Drugs as a Test

All adolescents engage in certain kinds of self-testing. Most of it takes conventional forms such as learning to drive a car, competing in sports, and experimenting with sex. Heavy drinking has long been favored and so too has marijuana smoking. But now alcohol and marijuana are so common that older youths in search of a way to prove themselves will often turn to stronger drugs—LSD, cocaine, or the dangerously unpredictable Angel Dust (phencyclidine or PCP). The risk of bad trips, or even death, is alluring to some youths. To indulge in the potentially lethal use of dangerous drugs provides them with a sense of achievement they cannot get in other ways. The teenager who is the first to use heroin knows that it is dangerous and so do his or her friends, who may now stand in awe of his or her courage.

For some youths, just using drugs after school with their friends is not enough. They feel compelled to test themselves through an initiation into the street culture—a world of violence, crime, and disease. The outcome of this kind of testing is often tragic.

Drugs and Feelings of Inadequacy

A positive sense of one's worth is one of the most important anchors a person can possess. Children who

85

have positive views of themselves tend to act in ways that contribute to early success and bring further success. Children who have negative views of themselves are pessimistic about their futures. They tend to make halfhearted efforts because they feel they will fail anyway. Sometimes, these children turn to drugs.

Persons with low self-esteem are extremely sensitive to stress in their lives, and they feel compelled to defend themselves against insecurity. Such individuals move easily into drug use and abuse because, by either inducing feelings of well-being or by dulling the senses, drugs seem to provide relief from stress and to protect the self from feelings of inferiority. But because drugs only treat the symptoms and not the root problems, drug use only further increases a child's sense of failure, and a vicious cycle that requires even more drugs is established.

Drugs and Overachievers

Children who have low self-esteem because of repeated disappointments and frustrations in achieving goals are not the only ones with a sense of failure. Overachievers sometimes reach the same point. Some child-behavior experts contend that many children are being pushed too fast without sufficient parental support. Their parents expect them to excel in school, but they never support their efforts with attention and praise or attend school functions with them. Despite academic and social success, such "hurried" children feel they have not impressed their parents, and inwardly feel they have failed.

Sometimes these children compound their problem by setting goals that are unattainable. To an observer, the child is bright and successful; but because

86

the child's goals are unrealistic, he or she has no sense of achievement. The frustration of never being able to meet their own expectations can motivate such children to drop out of the competition.

For these overachievers, drug use can become an attractive form of relief. The feelings induced by drugs are not subject to inspection and judgment by parents or teachers. They cannot be compared to anyone else's feelings. The pleasurable experiences found in drugs do not have to live up to anyone's expectations, and, most important, they can be achieved without any effort.

The Magical Qualities of Drugs

Given the adolescent need to belong and to be tested, it's easy to see why an invitation to become part of an inner circle of sophisticates is nearly irresistible. Here is a magic circle, made up not merely of friends but of brothers and sisters, bonded by the sharing of an intimate experience. Here is a magic circle, from within which a previously confusing and "programmed" world seemingly begins to make more sense. Here is a magic circle, with an exclusive membership, secret rituals, secret meetings, secret deals, codewords, and, above all, the secret knowledge of what it feels like to be high, to be stoned.

We all have a need to belong and to be liked, and the adult world contains all kinds of ceremonies and societies, from the Kiwanis to the Ku Klux Klan. But this magic circle of drug users appeals to children because it bans adults and thus provides an armor that many children long for. It posts a notice that says, "You can't come in here, and you can't tell me what to do." This magic circle gives children a role to play and a clue about how to act, what to say, how to think. In short, it provides a base from which to shape an identity.

So, what's wrong with such a haven from the real world? Don't we all need one? The problem with drug use is that it encourages the natural reluctance of children to grow up. Drugs serve to stop time, to diminish the pull of necessity and the demands of the outside world. Drugs encourage passivity. They weave a seemingly protective cocoon around a young personality at a time when it needs to develop the coping skills necessary to survive in a complex world.

The cocoon temporarily creates a loving, nurturing protection. This explains why children who are heavy drug users become so passive and uncommunicative: they are focused on the pleasurable experiences of an inner world. Drugs serve as a shield for such youngsters. Only through drugs do they feel confident enough to explore and develop their personalities. They yearn for a "good trip," for a creative experience that will grant in one stroke what most parents have so painfully acquired—an adult personality, able to cope with and enjoy life.

If you're skeptical about this magical quality of drugs, consider the following account, related by a college student named Henry, of an experience with LSD, a drug that has become popular once again with a new generation of adolescent users.

> It was the second time I had done acid. The first time was on two hundred mikes [micrograms] or so. It was nice but nothing really spectacular. The second time I took seven or eight hundred mikes—I figured I'd really get a taste of what it was like. Within about twenty minutes I could begin to feel the acid on the top of my spine, and a very subtle tingling in my fingertips. In an hour I was totally zonked and still going up. Every object in the room was moving

around—it was wild. Then some guy suggested that we should go swimming in the Adams House pool. So we got the key and went in and, God, what an experience! I dived into the water and it just came up and embraced my whole body with this wonderful, sexual feeling. And as I swam, the lights sparkled on the water around my hands, and suddenly I was swimming through a sea of rubies and diamonds and emeralds. And then, a few minutes later, I took a deep breath, and dived underwater, clutched my arms around my knees and hung there, just hung there for centuries and centuries, I mean literally centuries, with no light and no sound except the distant humming of the pump that keeps the pool full.

It's absolutely futile to attempt to describe in English what that moment felt like. There was no boundary between me and the world. I was everything and everything was me. I had gone back in time—back into the womb, and back before I was even a single cell, when the atoms from which I was made were spread all over the universe. It sounds like a bunch of empty phrases, because it's absolutely impossible to describe to somebody who hasn't been there. It was just pure experience, man! Pure, unadulterated experience![7]

Aside from the obvious Freudian implications of Henry's trip to an underwater womb, he clearly felt he was experiencing a union with the cosmos into which his identity had been temporarily surrendered or lost.

How reassuring such a trip must be to one whose identity is confused. To unsure youngsters, such an experience promises the nirvana of eastern mystics, and promises that such a state can be achieved without the lifelong physical and mental discipline mystics require. In short, drugs promise an escape—however unreal and illusory.

Drugs and Boredom

If drugs can hold out this sort of promise, it is small wonder that they appeal to ordinary kids who suffer from ordinary boredom. As Harrison Pope, who related Henry's LSD experience, said about the properties of LSD, "If a high school student is aware of this (as many are) and feeling rather bored of an evening, what will he do? He can watch TV, go for a ride with his friends, study math, take a date to the hamburger stand, or for the five-second effort of swallowing two tablets, he might have Henry's experience in the pool."[8]

The adolescent complaint about boredom puzzles and irritates many adults. After all, most American youngsters have opportunities for education and amusement that were unheard of even fifty years ago—and that are still beyond the reach of most of the world's citizens. But affluence can create its own problems, too. Sometimes when teenagers complain that "There's nothing to do," they mean, "There's nothing *essential* to do."

Adolescents can be responsible and energetic—anything but bored—when they sense their efforts are truly needed. But often they are expected to contribute little more to the family than occasional chores. In many middle-class homes, they are trained to be consumers and to amuse themselves with sophisticated toys, sports equipment, and TV.

Some people blame television for altering an entire generation's ability to read, to concentrate, to play creatively, or to develop other powers of the mind. In an insightful book about television and children entitled *The Plug-In Drug,* Marie Winn observes that television watching approaches a state of "pure awareness'' similar to that often described by drug users. This is a state in which "the person is completely and vividly aware of his experience, but there are no processes of thinking, manipulating, or interpreting going on. The sensations fill the person's attention, which is passive, but absorbed in what is occurring, which is usually experienced as intense and immediate. Pure awareness is experiencing without associations to what is there.''[9]

If one of Winn's main observations is accurate— that what you watch is nowhere nearly as important as the act of watching itself—TV may be far less educational than its creators hoped it would be. And it may well be depriving children of the opportunity to engage in the necessary intellectual exploration that contributes to maturity.

With fewer intellectual resources, are children more easily bored? In any case, drugs have provided an effortless outlet for many youngsters who are bored and seemingly incapable of an active mental life. Here are the words of one young drug user:

> My folks said, "What do you mean you have nothing to do? You have school, and you might be on the basketball team, and you have lots of books and your own TV set, and we let you use the car all the time." They went on and on like that, giving me five hundred irrefutable reasons why there must be something wrong with me if I was bored. And then I remember my mother saying, "Maybe you should see a psychiatrist a couple of times; it would help you out." They'd given me the car and bought me the TV set, so now they were going to buy me a psychiatrist to put me back in shape again. How can you talk to people like that? How can you possibly explain to them that until drugs came along, there was nothing in this dump that was really, that was really, fun?[10]

Drugs and Unhappy Family Life

Not all bored children will experiment with drugs. Young people who are reasonably at peace with themselves and their families and who are interested in the world around them and their own future seldom become seriously involved with drugs. But to the more apathetic and alienated, drugs become much more intriguing.

There is a fairly clear relationship between drug use and lack of parental control and support. If you suspect your child is using drugs, you should consider what part you might be playing in this development.

Many children who turn to drugs are not only bored but lonely—lonely for meaningful adult company. In the past, when families were less mobile, a child had many adults living close by, or even in the same house, to whom he or she could turn for understanding, advice, and support. An alcoholic, abusive father was less of a psychological disaster to a boy with a stalwart uncle to look up to. And a child with a neurotic and overly critical mother often could turn to a warmhearted, accepting grandmother or aunt.

Although this is still true for those with extended families, today's mobility and unstable family patterns have imposed a special kind of isolation upon many children. Today, a typical American family consists of Mom and Dad and the kids—and often just Mom *or* Dad and the kids. If one parent is indifferent, or too busy, or destructive, it creates a serious problem for a child, and two such parents can be a catastrophe.

In the face of such family difficulties, children often turn to their friends for the support that in past times they would normally have received from community and family relationships. Unfortunately, the

92

contemporaries to whom such children turn also lack experience and maturity. The result is a curious sort of solidarity that overidentifies with pop heroes in music, films, and the like. It is a solidarity often accompanied by a self-destructive desire to punish neglectful parents by wilder and wilder involvement with drugs, drinking, and sex.

A recent report by the White House Conference on Children had this to say about the vacuum left by a lack of adult influence on children:

> The isolation of children from adults simultaneously threatens the growth of the individual and the survival of the society. The young cannot pull themselves up by their own bootstraps. And it is primarily through observing, playing, and working with others older and younger than himself that a child discovers both what he can do and who he can become—that he develops both his ability and his identity. It is primarily through exposure and interaction with adults and children of different ages that a child acquires new interests and skills and learns the meaning of tolerance, cooperation, and compassion.[11]

The Hidden Messages in Drug Users' Behavior

Parents who provide inadequate examples or communicate poorly will probably create problems for their children. A problem home is one of the first things a professional counselor looks for. But poor family relationships are rarely the only reason for a child's drug use. As we have seen, many factors can enter in, and drug counselors often see an interweaving of these factors.

Here's one boy's recollection of his early en-

counters with drugs. He is an only child who eventually dropped out of high school. If you were a drug
counselor, what might you see in these remarks that
reveal the boy's problems with his family and his reasons for turning to drugs?

> In the summers my family used to go to the
> beach where we had this summer cottage. All my
> parents wanted was to be alone and do nothing.
> They'd sit around the house and work on home im-
> provements or drink, and I would go swimming. And
> after the first day of swimming, it got to be a real
> bummer. There just wasn't anything to do, except go
> around and look for the action, which never existed
> anyway. And then in the summer after ninth grade,
> some of my friends down there got some dope, and
> we would turn on down on the beach at night while
> my parents were drinking back at home. A couple of
> times we even smoked in the cottage upstairs from
> them, but of course they were too smashed to notice
> anything strange. Those times were really beautiful.
> There was a real sense of a bond between the kids
> there, a real sense of fraternity—it was beautiful.[12]

What messages do you find in the boy's story?
We see a child resentful of his parents and bent on
getting even with them for neglecting him. He imitates
their habit of getting "smashed," although he uses
pot instead of booze. He turns to friends for support
and creates a secret group of initiates who use the
excitement of illicit fun to relieve their boredom. The
members of the group find in drug use a magical sense
of companionship, a meaning, "a real sense of a
bond."

This boy's experience underlines the truly powerful role drugs have come to play in the lives of
adolescents. Twenty years ago, a bored and frustrated
youngster on vacation might at worst have engaged in

some vandalism or some drinking with friends. At best he might have spent the days sailing or reading or exploring, or simply suffering through a long and boring summer.

But today drugs have added a new dimension to adolescent life. In effect, drug use constitutes a new means of expression for children. Understanding what kids are saying, and coming to grips with some of the causes of drug use, is the first step in leading our children toward alternative behaviors that will help them become the finest adults they are capable of becoming.

Footnotes

[1] Robert Coram and Charlene Smith-Williams, Atlanta *Constitution,* December 17, 1980, 18A p. 1A.

[2] Harrison Pope, *Voices From the Drug Culture* (Boston: Beacon Press, 1971), p. 15.

[3] Hardin B. Jones and Helen C. Jones, *Sensual Drugs* (New York: Cambridge University Press, 1977).

[4] Robert Coram and Charlene Smith-Williams, Atlanta *Constitution,* December 17, 1980, 18A p. 1A.

[5] John Barbour, St. Paul *Pioneer Press,* March 16, 1981, p. 10.

[6] Pope, p. 72.

[7] Pope, pp. 29-30.

[8] Pope, p. 30.

[9] Marie Winn, *The Plug-In Drug* (New York: Viking Press, 1977), p. 112.

[10] Pope, p. 17.

[11] *Report to the President: White House Conference on Children* (Washington, DC: GPO, 1971), p. 242.

[12] Pope, p. 19.

8
A REALISTIC APPROACH TO THE PREVENTION OF DRUG USE

Prevention: Children and Drugs Don't Mix

One thing is certain: adolescents need to be prevented from using drugs. Drug use can retard maturation. It can hinder development of a capable personality, fostering instead an immature, insecure, and unstable youth unequipped for adulthood. In short, children who develop a dependency on drugs more often than not fail to learn how to cope with success and failure—and consequently fail to make the most of themselves.

But what can be done? How can we prevent children from succumbing to the lure of getting high? To many perplexed parents the widespread use of drugs seems an unprecedented form of mass derangement. But the truth is that for millions of youngsters drugs are fulfilling a need for pleasure and relief from adolescent problems that is otherwise not being adequately fulfilled.

As we have said, drug taking is behavior, and when drugs offer fun and other rewards, children may repeat the experience until it becomes habitual. Like other habits, drug dependence can be unlearned. But how much better it would be if children never learned it to begin with. The most effective form of drug prevention is that which prevents drug-use patterns from developing in the first place.

Prevention: Understanding Drug Use

Any parent who wants to help his or her children resist drugs must understand something about the pressures children face. Earlier we discussed some of these pressures. In general they stem from the fact that America is a materialistic, goal-oriented society— placing great emphasis on competitiveness, individual achievement, rational conduct, and technological thinking; believing strongly in the work ethic. This often results in inhibited emotions, deferred personal satisfaction and reward, and feelings of discontent.

Use of psychoactive drugs is in many respects a response to pressure. For example, stimulants provide high energy and intensified abilities; depressants permit less ambitious or capable individuals to withdraw from competition; hallucinogens, which provide multiple versions of reality, offer the rebellious a means to challenge society's insistence upon order and rationality. But drugs are not only a way to escape the demands of a high-powered society or the frustrations of an unhappy family life. Among older youths especially, drugs are also a way to cope with the depressing effects of being without a job or the hope of one, or of having a meaningless job and little chance of finding a better one.

Furthermore, many of our traditional values have themselves undergone change over the past several decades. Changes in political and social beliefs, in life-styles and sexual mores, have all challenged traditional authority and restrictions on behavior. Drug use is an extension of this challenge, and it is little wonder that it is often perceived as a threat to established order.

Prevention: Altering Social Attitudes Toward Drug Use

Anyone who wishes to help prevent drug use must keep in mind that drugs have become part of American society, and that prevention will never occur until social attitudes toward drug use change. Furthermore, drug abuse is impossible to eradicate entirely; some will always abuse drugs. The goal of prevention is to significantly reduce the proportions.

We have come a long way since the 1960's, when the dramatic increase in drug use began, toward understanding the causes and treatment of adolescent drug abuse. Much misinformation has been corrected, and we have begun to forge realistic policies to deal with the problem. But we have a long way to go. A malady so deeply imbedded in our cultural life cannot be cured merely by rehabilitating abusers or by locking them up. Instead, we need to understand the role drugs play in American society, and we need to change social attitudes and values so that fewer young people use drugs.

Prevention: Supply and Demand

Society has attempted to address the drug problem by enforcing laws against manufacture, sale, and possession; by treating abusers; and by educating youth. Most of the emphasis has been on law enforcement, but the results have been mixed. Reducing the *supply* of psychoactive substances is an obvious way of curtailing use. But it does little to alter the *demand* for drugs. Critics of our present prevention tactics point out that tightening up on drug supplies enriches the drug dealers and causes the crime rate to rise as drug prices rise. The fact is that the drug problem in America is a problem of demand, not supply. Our experience with Prohibition from 1920 to 1933 is the best example of the difficulty of eliminating the use of a drug that is well entrenched in society. That "noble experiment" didn't work because alcohol was in high demand by large segments of society. Attempts to enforce the law were such dismal failures that the Prohibition amendment was ultimately repealed.

So, although enforcement efforts are necessary to check abuse, they can't solve the problem by themselves. Neither can treatment programs, which are utilized only *after* drug use has done its damage. Drug-education programs in the schools can be effective, although they are sometimes ill-designed or ineffectually presented.

To find a solution to this difficult problem, parents and others must recognize the cultural and economic roots of drug abuse and then work toward social changes that ultimately will help make drug use unappealing.

Prevention: A Realistic Approach

How can this be done? Prevention must focus on the values of children and adolescents. By providing sensible drug education, by preparing children to cope with success and failure, by helping them become self-reliant, by helping them create satisfying alternative activities, by helping develop neighborhood and community networks of concerned families and friends, parents can promote an environment in which young people can grow up without turning to drugs.

It may sound old-fashioned, but parental influence is still the most important element in the development of a youngster's personality, and to a large extent it determines whether he or she will become a drug user. The first line of defense against use is the home. There a child can be best taught the hazards of use, and there strong family relationships can give a child important social skills and a positive self-image.

Prevention: Bringing Drug Education Home

The prevention of drug use begins in the home, and it should begin early. A parent should find opportunities to talk about drug use and its consequences from the time that a child enters school, and regular discussions should be continued throughout the adolescent years. Such talks should keep pace with your child's curiosity about drugs, increasing in detail and complexity as the child's understanding matures.

Children are naturally curious about drugs. You need to acquaint them and yourself with the reasons drugs are taken and why they can be very harmful. Explain the effects drugs have on children. Help your child understand that normal adolescence includes physical changes, psychological conflicts, sexual urges, and fluctuating moods; and emphasize the importance of not permitting drugs to interfere with learning to manage these experiences. Make it clear that learning to handle pressure, to cope with depression, to endure frustration, and to survive loneliness and pain are experiences that help a child mature into healthy adulthood—and that if drugs are used as crutches, he or she may never make it. Furthermore, the child should know that chronic use can also take a heavy physical toll on still-growing and developing bodies.

Parents can make a difference when a child is faced with a decision to use drugs or not. A child who is given an opportunity for self-expression and a feeling of self-worth in a home where there is love, responsibility, respect, and open communication is far less susceptible to drug use. How can you work toward more healthy and meaningful family relationships? As concerned parents, you might want to ask yourself the following questions.

AM I WILLING TO TALK TO MY CHILD ABOUT DRUGS?

Try to keep drugs an open topic of conversation. You don't need to be an expert to have a discussion with your child. Simply communicating your desire to learn more about drugs, or a specific drug-related topic, is sometimes a good beginning point for a conversation. And a subtle approach is far more effective than a tirade. Don't try to "rap" or use street slang with your child. You're probably not up to date on the latest expressions, and you may sound ridiculous.

For many youngsters, drugs are a fascinating subject. Some children are budding pharmacologists and physiologists who bring an intensity to their study of psychoactive substances that would amaze their science teachers. But these amateur researchers, even those who are cautious about their drug use, can and do make mistakes. Unfortunately, many such adolescent users view adults with suspicion and hostility,

101

and they are quick to reject attempts by adults to talk to them about the actions and consequences of illicit drugs.

Most children, however, are not very confident about their knowledge of the effects of drugs. They are in need of credible information, and informed parents can help educate them. Parents can get information about drugs and the drug scene from a number of sources. Local drug-abuse programs, public and university libraries, and federal and state government programs and publications provide useful information. Even a story in your newspaper or on the evening news can sometimes serve as a stimulus for a discussion of drug use. You might ask your child if he or she thinks the story is biased, oversimplified, or exaggerated. The response may tell you something about how well informed he or she is, and it may show you that there is a difference in perception between the reporter's version of drug use and that of your child's circle of friends.

In addition, look at the merchandise and reading material (publications such as *High Times*) available to your children at the local "head shop " These shops are often record stores that also sell papers and pipes for smoking marijuana as well as other drug-related paraphernalia. You can locate one by looking in the Yellow Pages under the heading RECORDS—PHONO-GRAPH—RETAIL. Head shops can usually be identified by their advertisements for smoking paraphernalia, incense, and the like.

AM I GIVING MY CHILD THE RIGHT KIND OF LOVE?

Many children use drugs when they do not feel loved and wanted. A child must sense that he or she is loved for what he or she *is,* not for what he or she may *become.* He or she should be shown early that love doesn't have to be *earned.* Expressing your love, affection, and acceptance without attaching strings can provide a child with the kind of security that goes far toward eliminating the need to use drugs.

AM I HELPING MY CHILD DEVELOP A POSITIVE SELF-IMAGE?

One of the major tasks of adolesence is to complete the process, begun early in life, of constructing a positive self-image. Children develop much of their self-esteem by listening to what parents and other adults say about them and by observing how grown-ups treat them. Children who are told that they never measure up or that they will never amount to anything may indeed fulfill a parent's poor expectations, and they may turn to drugs for comfort, centering their lives around them.

It is important to maintain positive but realistic expectations of your children and to let them know that you respect and value them for what they are. Children who are continually confronted with their mistakes often become overwhelmed by feelings of inadequacy. Youngsters need to know that you see their strengths, too, and that their efforts are valued, even though they don't always succeed. Remember, a child can have nothing more valuable than a good self-image.

AM I HELPING MY CHILD DEVELOP DECISION-MAKING SKILLS?

A responsible parent allows a child to make those decisions he or she is *competent* to make. A parent

103

who constantly makes a child's decisions for him or her is courting trouble. How can a child make a wise decision about drugs if he or she has never been allowed to make decisions?

Parents attempting to help a teenager develop decision-making skills find themselves in a continual balancing act. On the one hand, rules must be set and limits defined. On the other, room must be allowed for children to grow and to make mistakes. But being too restrictive or too permissive robs children of the opportunity to learn how to make *responsible* decisions. Find the comfortable middle ground. With your child, establish reasonable rules and make sure he or she understands them. Concentrate on the important issues, such as knowing where he or she is and who he or she is with. And don't waste energy on insignificant issues. Arguments about them will only convince your child that you will never understand him or her.

AM I ENCOURAGING MY CHILD IN THE RIGHT WAYS?

Children need encouragement, but encouragement involves more than just praise for a child's achievements. Sometimes the wrong kind of praise can cause *discouragement,* especially if children feel it is undeserved or that even more is expected of them—more, perhaps, than they are capable of achieving. Make it clear that you are praising him or her for the decision to undertake a task and for the efforts to succeed at it rather than for the accomplishment itself. Encouragement means commending the *effort,* whether it is successful or not. Achievements are important; but to a child, the knowledge that his or her parents have confidence in his or her abilities is even more important. Such confidence encourages a child to keep trying, despite occasional failures. It helps put failure and success in perspective.

AM I HAVING FUN WITH MY CHILD?

Laughter and play can bring parents and children together in an easy way. Having fun together promotes feelings of love, affection, trust, and belonging. One useful way of having fun with your child is to share tasks that require concentration, effort, and cooperation. Playing, working, and sharing everyday experiences teach a child to value work, achievement, and cooperation. Such shared and pleasurable activities can lead to the kind of family closeness that produces a self-reliant and well-adjusted child who will find drugs less attractive. So spend time with your child and enjoy each other. The investment can have a big payoff.

AM I HELPING MY CHILD DEVELOP ALTERNATIVES TO DRUG USE?

The development of alternatives to drug use can be a highly effective approach to prevention. Alternatives help fulfill needs that otherwise might be met through drug use. Adolescents have enormous reservoirs of energy and enthusiasm for which they need outlets. Development of skills and hobbies such as photography or the development of creative talents in music, acting, and painting, or participation in sports, are examples of such alternatives.

Children also welcome opportunities to contrib-

ute something positive to their communities, something that goes beyond their personal needs. This need
for community involvement is often met by the thousands of local and national organizations such as the
Boy Scouts, Girl Scouts, Boys' Clubs, 4-H clubs, the
YMCAs, YWCAs, etc. All these groups provide a
wide range of recreational and social activities that
offer alternatives to drug use.

However, such youth organizations cannot reach
all youths. For this reason, many communities have
developed projects of their own. Typical of these are
a youth-run project for restoring historical sites, a program enlisting high school students as counselors in a
day-care camp for the physically handicapped, an eth-
nic dance group for black teenagers, an inner-city program that enables former delinquents to tutor other
youths, and a school-based program in which teenagers do ecological field work.

Young participants in these programs and the
specialists who developed them agree they work because they generate their own pleasure, and they offer
the kind of positive experiences that make drugs less
interesting. Such alternatives provide more than just
a substitute for drugs; they yield more real satisfaction
than drugs. The alternative can take many forms—
boxing or ballet, stargazing or bird-watching, cos-
metology or oceanography, computer electronics or
astrophysics, stock cars or the stock market. The important point is that a child discovers he or she can
achieve a passionate interest in some project.

When opportunities to pursue worthwhile goals
are made available, children often surprise even the
most skeptical parents with the energy and enthusiasm
they bring to the project. A child who experiences the
excitement of being absorbed in a new subject is far
less likely to be bored and self-doubting. And in the

challenge of the project, he or she learns more about independence, responsibility, discipline, and achievement than parental lectures could ever teach. But a child who lacks such experiences tends to think less of himself or herself and may risk taking drugs because of it.

Prevention: Organizing for Parent Power

In many parts of the country, parents are establishing neighborhood and community-wide drug-abuse prevention programs. They are showing that parent power works and that parents *can* make a difference. Although your child is exposed daily to drugs, you can minimize the risk of his or her getting caught up in them. You *can* take action. By joining other concerned adults in your community, you can greatly reduce both your child's desire to use drugs and his or her opportunities to do so. You can help your child learn to say no to drugs. As many parent groups around the country have discovered, organizing to combat drug use has many advantages:

- It brings the problem of drug use into the open. For parents who are ashamed of their children's drug use, the knowledge that their neighbors are dealing with the same problems can relieve tension and stir action.
- It clarifies the scope of the problem and allows a realistic appraisal of it.
- Parents become better informed about drugs and their effects and about the role of drugs in the community. They become more aware of how society encourages the use of drugs, and they learn to identify problems, such as the presence of head shops or particular children who promote use in their neighborhood.

107

• Discussion of their children's drug use makes parents more aware of their own. They begin to see how their attitudes influence their children, and they often become more responsible.

• The development of consistent rules and expectations in a neighborhood makes the rules and expectations easier to enforce. Consequently, it is easier for children to resist the pressures that push them toward drug use.

• Through a united front, parents develop confidence in their ability to stop the spread of drugs in a neighborhood, and they begin to think about community-wide prevention efforts.

• Neighborhood ties are strengthened as parents exchange information and advice about common problems.

• Family life is enhanced as parents learn about programs for strengthening the family, improving parenting and communication skills, and developing alternatives to drug use.

Prevention: How One Community Organized Against Adolescent Drug Use

Each community is different, and each must respond to the problem of adolescent drug use in its own way. Although there is no simple formula for establishing a drug-abuse prevention program, many communities are pooling state, local, and private resources to effectively counteract the incursion of drugs into their schools and neighborhoods. Here is a brief description of how four communities organized themselves.

In the spring of 1979, parents, school officials, clergymen, the mayors and police chiefs from four neighboring Minnesota communities with a total population of some thirty thousand met to finalize plans to establish a drug-abuse prevention program. This program was designed to provide drug education in the schools and in the community, to establish alternative activities for children, and to help individuals and families with drug problems. With funding and advice from state, county, and private sources, the program set up a citizen advisory committee, hired a school and a community coordinator, and began creating numerous workshops and seminars that schoolchildren and their families were urged to attend.

By the fall of 1981, a variety of lectures, classes, and workshops featuring films, guest speakers, demonstrations, and discussions had been developed and were being offered to the community. Among those open to parents were sessions on successful parenting, how to talk to children about drinking, marijuana use, and responsible hosting of parties. Parents and their children participated in drug-awareness workshops and other sessions devoted to improving communication skills, resolving conflicts, and making responsible decisions about drug use.

The programs in the elementary and secondary schools were coordinated to prepare children for exposure to drugs. They offered children sensible information about drugs; and they promoted discussion of such issues as healthy living, how to form a positive self-concept, peer pressures and how to manage them, how to resolve conflicts, how to manage emotions, and alternatives to drug use.

The four communities' response to this program has been very positive, and their citizens have been drawn together as a result of it. A recent survey revealed that the program is considered a success and an integral part of the life of the communities. One participating resident commented:

> My approach to drug problems is more confident and understanding now. There are no simple

answers or guarantees to these problems, but being involved and being informed will help us guide our children through difficult times. I have an awareness of the tremendous focus on chemicals in our culture to make us "feel better." Also, I see the importance of good family relationships to develop a good self-concept within the child as one of the most effective prevention measures. The whole "drug problem" was a dark mystery before; now I can see it as one of the human problems that everyone faces.

Prevention: The National Federation of Parents for Drug-Free Youth

In May 1980, 370 parent groups ranging in size from four to five families up to community-wide organizations of several thousand members formed the National Federation of Parents for Drug-Free Youth (NFP). NFP offers direct assistance to parents who are organizing community-action programs. Upon written request, they will provide the names of speakers who are authorities on the medical, legal, and legislative issues surrounding illicit drug use. In addition, the NFP provides ongoing consultation services for parents who are developing community drug-abuse prevention programs. They also publish a monthly newsletter that provides up-to-date information about drug-related issues and the activities of parent groups around the country. And the NFP resource list contains numerous publications and other materials—pamphlets, leaflets, flyers, brochures, films, information kits—that can assist parents in developing prevention programs. For information, write or call:

National Federation of Parents for Drug-Free Youth
9805 Dameron Drive
Silver Spring, MD 20902
(301) 593-9256

110

Prevention: Other Useful Publications

Parents, Peers, and Pot (free)
National Institute on Drug Abuse
P.O. Box 1909
Rockville, MD 20850

How to Form a Families-in-Action Group in Your Community ($10)
Families in Action
P.O. Box 15053
Atlanta, GA 30333

California Parents for Action on Drug and Alcohol Abuse How-To Kit ($3)
P.O. Box 60962
Sacramento, CA 95860

Parent-Teen Guidelines ($1)
Unified Parents of America
P.O. Box 27585
Atlanta, GA 30327

Drug Paraphernalia Packet ($5)
Gerri Silverman
23 Audubon Court
Short Hills, NJ 07078

Stop the Drug Epidemic in Your Community With Effective Political Action ($4)
Interstate Movement Against Dangerous Drugs
P.O. Box 6272
Silver Spring, MD 20906

Model Drug Paraphernalia Law (free)
U.S. Drug Enforcement Administation
2405 "I" Street, NW
Washington, DC 30537

Quest (Alternatives to drug use)
2707 North Main
Findlay, OH 45840

How to Give a Drug-Free Party
Parents Who Care
P.O. Box 50663
Palo Alto, CA 94303

For Parents Only: What Kids Think About Marijuana
(Film and pamphlets produced by US Drug Abuse
Prevention Agency—available free)
Modern Talking Picture Service
5000 Park Street North
St. Petersburg, FL 33709

Prevention: Can Parents Effect Social Change?

Social change comes about slowly and usually through the concerted efforts of millions of people working toward a common goal. Changing social values is a difficult undertaking, but it is not an impossible one. It begins with a personal decision to do something. Once you recognize that apathy and defeatism impede efforts to change social attitudes, you can organize parents to combat drug use in your neighborhood.

And once you have an effective neighborhood organization, you can widen your horizons. How? By applying pressure. The pressure brought to bear by organized interest groups is at the heart of the American political system. From abolitionists to present-day civil rights advocates, from oil lobbyists to conservationists, from pro-life to pro-choice, and from Moral Majority to Common Cause, various groups of Americans have traditionally banded together to make their demands heard. Parent organizations can employ the same techniques to change social attitudes about *all* forms of drug use.

Who should be the target of parent group pressure? Parent groups can lobby media advertisers, television-program sponsors, television networks, and drug companies to eliminate or at least reduce the representation of alcohol, cigarettes, and over-the-counter drugs as substances that enhance pleasurable activities or that provide quick and powerful relief. Parent groups can remind the medical profession and the public about the dangers of unnecessarily prescribed drugs. They can impress upon sports and entertainment figures the need to present drug-free models to young people. They can ensure that local politicians and law enforcement authorities are informed about the nature and dimensions of the drug-use problem. And by combining efforts with other parent groups around the country, they can influence state and federal drug-abuse prevention policies. In short, parents *can* do something about adolescent drug use in America, and furthermore, they can determine how it is to be done.

9
WHAT ARE DRUGS?

What Is a Drug?

Broadly defined, a drug is any substance whose chemical makeup interacts with the chemical makeup of a living organism in a way that alters the physiological and/or psychological behavior of the organism.

What is Drug Use?

As chemicals, drugs are neither good nor bad. Their value depends on the way they are used. We label drugs as medicine when we use them to treat illness or disease. In such cases, we think of drugs as substances that make sick people healthy. But when the body has no medical need for drugs, we think of them as substances that make healthy people sick.

Many drugs such as laxatives, diet pills, or indigestion tablets are misused by hypochondriacs or others ill-informed about how to use their medications. The misuse of aspirin accounts for many injuries and deaths each year. But such misuse generally occurs in the mistaken belief that excessive use of these drugs will restore health. The aim of such misguided use is relief, not pleasure.

114

But the motive for drug use is different for those whom we call drug experimenters, recreational drug users, drug abusers, drug addicts, or chemically dependent persons. In their cases, the first aim in taking drugs is pleasure, not health. Thus it is that when we talk about a drug problem we are really talking about a behavior problem. That is, it is behavior, not drugs, that is the problem. With this distinction in mind, we can add a further definition: nonmedical drug use is the taking of a chemical substance into the body with the *intention* of altering healthy physiological functioning and normal psychological behavior.

How Do Drugs Work?

The body is able to maintain a normal chemical balance as long as it has an adequate diet and remains disease-free and uninjured. This balance is maintained chiefly through the action of the brain, an extraordinarily complex and delicate mechanism. The human brain has some ten billion nerve cells that comprise approximately ninety percent of all the cells in the body's nervous system.

This compact structure is arranged into elaborate control systems that keep all body functions operating within a normal range. Communication along the nerve pathways that transmit sensory information to the brain and return the brain's responses depends upon the proper functioning of electrochemical charges that flow through these billions of nerve cells.

The brain, in other words, is completely dependent upon a correct chemical balance. As the human brain has evolved over millions of years, its control centers have become more complex, so that a small alteration in one often profoundly affects a vast num-

115

ber of others. Thus, when the brain's control centers release or inhibit the dozens of hormones and thousands of enzymes that regulate body functions, growth, and metabolism, they are adjusting the body's chemistry by a process of extraordinary fine tuning.

When disease or injury interfere with the healthy functioning of the body, this chemical balance is altered, and symptoms appear to warn us of the altered condition. Although the body has remarkable self-healing powers, we have discovered that various chemicals can also help restore the normal physio-chemical functions of the body.

Many chemicals that are introduced into the body are able to enter the brain through the bloodstream. Regardless of whether a drug is taken to relieve a stomachache or to cure malaria, its active chemicals very often have an effect on more than one site in the body, for many drugs affect the control centers responsible for chemical balance throughout the body.

The brain responds to the presence of new chemicals by trying to adjust the body's systems to a normal, healthy state. As Dr. Hardin Jones points out in *Sensual Drugs,* his study of drugs and the brain, we now have drugs that can cause the brain to raise and lower blood pressure, increase or decrease the heartbeat, alter body temperature, cause blood to thin or coagulate, dilate or contract the arteries, release or inhibit body fluids or secretions, anesthetize generally or locally—and control and alter moods.[1]

How Do Drugs Affect the Mind?

Many drugs and other chemical substances (such as those present in the foods we eat) can affect our mental functioning and our moods. Normally, brain functions are affected by external stimuli—the things we see, hear, touch, taste, or smell—or by internal sensations of pain or pleasure. But similar reactions can be produced when the chemicals in various drugs find their way into the brain.

For example, the brain operates the autonomic nervous system, which regulates many of the body's internal functions. This system is made up of two complementary subsystems: the sympathetic nervous system, which, in general terms, controls the body's response to excitement, and the parasympathetic nervous system, which calms and relaxes the body. Increases or decreases in adrenaline, thyroxin, cortisone, and other hormonal secretions that affect our moods, are regulated by these two coordinated parts of the autonomic nervous system.

The point of this physiology lesson is that control centers of the brain affect our moods by chemical regulation. This may seem a novel way of describing what we call our feelings. Most of us think of our feelings as "states of mind." When we are depressed, unhappy, or bored, or pleased, glad, or elated, we experience emotions that occur in what we call our *minds*. We simply take for granted the notion that our consciousness is somehow contained in our heads, but that it is not a thing that one can take out and examine under a microscope.

But psychologists and others who study the phenomena of consciousness know that consciousness is the end result of an extraordinarily complex arrangement of biochemical interactions in the brain. Our moods and feelings are products of thousands of interrelated chemical changes in the tissues of the brain. The same is true, of course, for our thoughts and our reasoning abilities, our memories, imaginations and dreams, and other products of our conscious and un-

117

conscious minds. Chemistry is literally the core of our psychic existences.

Why Do Some Drugs Alter the Mind More Than Others?

The mind is a neurochemical entity: this is why certain chemicals in drugs can so powerfully affect our minds. Although most drugs act on the brain as well as the body, some drugs affect more than others the chemical balances responsible for mental functioning. In some cases, the effect occurs because certain drugs fool the brain by mimicking naturally produced chemicals. In other cases, drugs compete with these naturally produced chemicals and block normal nerve cell function.

For instance, one of the more exciting findings of recent neurochemical research is the discovery that all animals, including man, produce their own pain-relieving and pleasure-inducing chemicals.

These chemicals are called *enkephalins* and *endorphins*. They act on the central nervous system in much the same way as opiate narcotics such as morphine and heroin. When produced by the body in response to pain or anguish, they occupy the same nerve cell receptor sites as the opium-derived narcotics. The result is that nerve cells that are occupied by either enkephalins or narcotics inhibit or modulate the excitation that normally signals pain or unpleasant emotion.

Endorphins are thought to be responsible, for example, for the phenomenon known to some joggers as *runner's high*—a feeling of extreme well-being that occurs toward the end of a long run. This sensation often produces an "addiction" to running to which

118

runners and non-running spouses alike can testify. Conversely, low levels of enkephalins are suspected of contributing to psychological depression.

This chemical similarity between internally produced ''opiates'' and narcotics derived from the opium poppy is a likely explanation for the powerful pain-killing properties of morphine, as well as for the euphoria that accompanies heroin use. These and other drugs that directly affect areas of the brain that control moods and mental processes are often called *psychoactive drugs*.

Psychoactive drugs generally alter the normal stimulus-and-response relationship of the autonomic nervous system. They also affect other body systems as well, since, like other drugs, they accumulate in the liver, kidneys, and intestines, where they are metabolized and excreted. Psychoactive drugs can and do cause damage to these other body organs, but their primary effects are on the neurochemical balance of the brain's delicate communication network.

Why Are Certain Mind-Altering Drugs Preferred by Drug Users?

There are numerous psychoactive drugs, but not all of them are selected by drug users deliberately seeking an altered state of mind. For example, the group of drugs known as the major tranquilizers has not become part of the drug user's repertoire. Although they clearly affect the moods and mental functioning of patients to whom they are administered, no one gets ''hooked'' on such anti-schizophrenic tranquilizers as Thorazine, Mellaril, Stelazine, or Haldol.

Why is it, then, that of the many drugs capable of altering brain chemistry, only certain ones are

119

sought by drug users? The answer seems to be that these psychoactive drugs preferred by drug users stimulate those regions of the brain that control the production of pleasurable sensations.

These pleasure control centers are normally activated by sensory stimuli from what we see, hear, smell, touch, or taste—and by our thoughts. Our thoughts often affect our responses. For example, many of the pleasures of drug use must be learned. The body's initial responses—such as dizziness or hallucinations—to the unpleasant effects of some drugs must be interpreted as pleasurable. The novice drug user's expectations are often influenced by a more experienced user's guidance.

Although not much is known about just how the brain produces pleasurable sensations, we do know that it does, and we know where these pleasure sectors are located. Experiments with laboratory animals and humans have demonstrated that an area of the brain known as the *limbic region* can be artifically stimulated to produce intense pleasure by either mild electrical current or the application of various chemicals, including pleasure-inducing drugs.

The limbic region is a major part of the brain, and it strongly influences the autonomic nervous system and internal organs such as the heart, lungs, liver, and intestines. It is involved in a variety of other physiological functions such as memory storage and the generation of intense emotions, and it also exerts control over various drives, including the sexual drive.

It is this last function, the generation of sexual pleasure, that is often overlooked in discussions about drugs and drug use. Many of the effects of the psychoactive drugs that are chosen by drug users are similar to, and often more intense than, pleasurable sexual

120

sensations. Intense excitement, feelings of warmth in the abdomen and elsewhere, rushes of pleasure, and occasionally the actual arousal of the sex organs or the deep relaxation and mild euphoric feelings characteristic of post-orgasmic relaxation, are sensations that accompany the use of a number of psychoactive drugs. (To illustrate the complexity of neurochemical brain activity, many heroin addicts report that they experience sexual feelings at the mere sight of a hypodermic syringe—and also that the act of injection itself can be pleasurable.)

Not all drugs are taken to achieve these specific feelings of sexual pleasure, but these effects are present to some degree in the responses that drugs simulate in the brain, and it is these effects that give rise to the belief that some drugs are aphrodisiacs.

Although the association of pleasure with chemistry may seem odd at first glance, it should be clear from what we have said about drugs and the brain that it is this connection that accounts for a drug user's choices. We can now add another definition to our list: preferred psychoactive drugs are chemical substances whose primary effect is on the pleasure control centers of the brain.

What's Wrong With Using Drugs?

You should now understand that drugs taken by a healthy person alter the chemical balance of the brain and the body. How damaging is this? Is it damaging at all? The answers to these questions depend on four factors: the size of the dose, the strength of the active chemical ingredients, the regularity with which the drug is taken, and the duration of regular use.

121

Any chemical, from arsenic to zinc, can alter body chemistry, and the body's controls will try to bring the chemical balance back to a state of equilibrium as soon as a foreign substance is detected. *Psychoactive drugs, like any other drugs, have to be considered as potential poisons.*

Is It Ever Safe to Use Drugs?

What are the risks for a drug user who occasionally indulges moderately? People who occasionally have a drink or who smoke marijuana now and then do not seem to have long-term ill effects. A first-time user of cocaine, amphetamines, barbiturates, or heroin is not likely to suffer from any physical or psychological dependence. Although it is not possible to state categorically that there is no subtle damage to cellular structure from infrequent low doses, physiologically the brain and other body cells will probably recover from the temporary imbalance caused by such use.

The risk of incurring long-term or even irreversible effects increases with increased dosage and frequency of use. In other words, the risk factor increases with repetition, and the effortless pleasure psychoactive drugs can deliver is a powerful incentive to repeat the experience.

Drug use is a risk-taking activity. Some drugs are obviously more dangerous than others. But *all* psychoactive drugs have a demonstrated capacity for causing harm, and it is rational to conclude that the user is risking his or her health and life by using them. Realistically, drugs are a part of life, and some, like alcohol and tobacco, are a part of the social life of many people. But their use nevertheless involves risks that should not be taken lightly.

122

What Are the Risks of Drug Use?

Although we have focused so far on the action of drugs on the brain, the toxic effects of psychoactive drugs can affect many other sites. It is well known that alcohol also attacks the liver, as does heavy use of amphetamines, marijuana, and inhaled volatile solvents. It is beyond dispute that both tobacco and marijuana smoke can have severe effects on the respiratory system. Many other health disorders attend drug use: dirty needles can cause abscesses and can transmit kidney, liver, and venereal diseases; cocaine and amphetamine snorting can destroy nasal membranes and cause hair to fall out; unborn babies can suffer opiate addiction and withdrawal symptoms; the self-neglect and poor nutrition of most heavy drug users make them susceptible to pneumonia and tuberculosis; and, of course, an overdose of any drug can be fatal, as can drug-related auto accidents or drug-induced violent behavior.

An increasingly dangerous problem for drug users is toxic reaction from the use of impure street drugs. As one researcher, Dr. Samuel Irwin, in *Drugs of Abuse,* has noted:

> Most of the pills, capsules, and powders prepared and sold illicitly are done so with little regard for human safety. The level of fraud in the illicit market is appalling, as is the evident lack of quality control over composition, dosage, and potential toxicity of most of the drugs sold, In consequence, one assumes considerable risk ingesting or injecting illicit substances. The greater the demand for the drug, obviously the more expensive it becomes and unfortunately the greater the risk of substitution or adulteration. All too often the drugs are not what they are

123

claimed to be, they contain too high a dose for safe use, or they are cut with chemicals intended to mimic a drug's action, chemicals which may have more dangerous potentials than the drug purported to be in the pill.[2]

Related to this problem is the recent appearance of "look-alikes"—pills and capsules that are made up of legally obtainable, over-the-counter substances that are packaged to look like other drugs, such as amphetamines. Although the individual ingredients of these look-alike compounds have relatively mild effects, in combination they are unpredictable and dangerous, especially in high doses. As these substances made their first appearances in 1980, severe overdose symptoms were reported, including massive brain hemorrhages and death. And a particulary vicious twist was added when users really did purchase amphetamines, and overdosed, thinking they were using the counterfeit compound.

The hazards of multiple-drug use are unquestionably great. Although the fatal effects of alcohol and barbiturate combinations have long been known, the mixing of other drugs has only begun to be studied, and its consequences are not yet known. Surveys indicate that the latest trend among adolescents is toward long-term use of both alcohol and marijuana in combination; but a recent nationwide study of adolescents in drug-treatment programs showed the average patient had not only used alcohol and marijuana but had "regularly abused approximately five other drugs prior to coming into treatment."[3]

Another hazard for drug users is sensory deprivation. As any smoker can tell you, the senses of smell and taste are diminished with constant drug use, as is even the ability to enjoy tobacco. Chronic drug use can suppress the normal experiences of pleasure

124

one receives from sensations and thought, until only the drug gives pleasure, and even that pleasure becomes fleeting as tolerance to the drug develops. With addicts, especially heroin addicts, this can lead to sexual dysfunction. Dr. Jones, whose rehabilitation strategy stresses an understanding of the close relationship between drug taking and sex, describes this process of sensory deprivation:

> The opiate user also experiences the loss of sexual capacity. Not only is the ability to feel sexual sensations suppressed, but the desire for sex is lost as well. The addict is able to retain the overwhelming pleasure of the opiate only because he increases the dose. When his senses fully tolerate the highest doses—when, as the addicts say, he is burned out— he is as unresponsive to opiates as he is to sex. No sensations can give him pleasure. An addict may undergo withdrawal so he can renew his sensitivity to opiates, but this does not fully restore his emotional or sexual powers. By the age of thirty-five, an addict may be totally unresponsive both to drugs and to normal emotions.[4]

Can Drugs Damage the Brain?

The dangers we have been discussing are significant. But it is the unbalancing effects on brain controls that are the trademark of psychoactive substances. As Dr. Jones notes in *Sensual Drugs,* the toxic shock to the autonomic nervous system is well illustrated by the effects of a drug like heroin:

> Breathing and pulse rate slow; blood pressure is reduced; blood-sugar levels are altered; urine excretion is increased; intestines have less movement; biliary and urinary tract sphincters are less responsive; body temperature is lowered; the eyes become red,

the pupils constrict, the eyelids droop, and vision becomes less acute; the release of pituitary hormones is
decreased; sweating may occur; pain is not bother-
some; the mind clouds.[5]

In spite of the immense difficulty of identifying
cell damage in such a highly complex structure as the
brain, with its billions of nerve cells and thousands of
nerve pathways, as Dr. Jones points out, "All psychoactive drugs, taken in large doses or frequently for
a long time, appear to produce toxic changes in the
brain that are detectable on microscopic examination."[6]

Most studies that have been done on brain cell
damage seem to agree that cells *can* recover from low
doses of such drugs; but with high doses or chronic
usage, sick brain cells may become dead brain cells.
Brain research can tell a chronic drug user that he or
she is risking diminished brain capacity, memory disorders, accelerated aging, anoxia (failing oxygen supplies to the brain), brain hemorrhage, disordered
thinking, impaired speech, and residual tremor, to
mention only a few kinds of damage that psychoactive
substances in toxic doses can inflict on the brain.
Common sense should tell a user that if one takes
chemicals to alter one's self, one runs the risk of being
altered.

What Is Drug Dependency?

A drug user who develops a continuous need for a
drug is said to be *chemically dependent* or *addicted*
to the drug. The possibility of developing a drug dependency is high on the list of risks for a drug user.
In some cases, the chemical imbalances have become
so chronic that the brain's control centers have ad-

justed to the drug's continuous presence, and a new balance is established. This phenomenon is often referred to as *physical dependency*. Physical dependency is signaled by *withdrawal symptoms* such as vomiting, tremors, sweating, insomnia, or even convulsions, if the drug is withdrawn from the system.

These symptoms are the result of the brain's attempt to restore chemical balance when the drug it has become accustomed to is unavailable. At this point, drugs are no longer taken primarily for pleasure; they have become necessary to maintain the drug user's artificial state and to prevent withdrawal symptoms.

Physical dependency is often distinguished from *psychological dependency,* which is characterized by a feeling of such intense desire for the drug that its use cannot be stopped or controlled without great difficulty. Withdrawal symptoms are more likely to be on an emotional level and marked by anguish, irritability, irrationality, anxiety, and restlessness.

But insofar as the brain has become dependent on the drug for stimulation of the pleasure centers, psychological dependency is as related to neurochemical factors as physical dependency. Thus the distinction between physical and psychological dependency is largely a semantic one. In real terms, the distinction matters very little to the dependent drug user. Psychological dependence is no less compelling and no less harmful to the user than physical dependence.

Tolerance is another consequence of chronic drug use. Tolerance to a specific drug occurs when the brain's control centers compensate for the presence of the drug, and the user must take more and more of the drug to achieve the same sensations. Some drugs provoke *reverse tolerance.* This can occur either when residues of the drug remain in the body (such as with the accumulation in the fatty tissues of THC, the active ingredient in marijuana), or when other organs

127

outside of the brain are no longer able to process as much of the drug (such as with liver damage in alcohol abuse).

A Commonsense Approach to the Hazards of Drugs

By now, we hope it is obvious to you that drugs have a great potential for damaging the brain as well as the body, and, if enough individuals suffer ill effects, for damaging society as well. This is a very sensitive issue: because the pleasure of drugs is so powerfully persuasive, drug users are very reluctant to acknowledge that they may be harming themselves. And some educators and others concerned with drug abuse often confuse the issue by overstating the case, claiming that any drug use causes irreparable damage.

We believe that anyone with common sense can understand two things about drugs: first, psychoactive drug use *can be* very hazardous; and, second, psychoactive drug abuse *is* a major social problem.

These things seem obvious. Alcoholism is a disease that not only kills millions through liver damage, heart disease, and auto deaths, but also destroys homelife. Millions more are victims of lung diseases brought on by smoking tobacco and marijuana.

The increasing use of other drugs diverts vast resources into wasteful and harmful avenues and results in an increasing need for drug education and drug-treatment centers.

The *amotivational syndrome*—the loss of interest in all activities except drug use—is often associated with heavy marijuana use and is an increasing source of tension within families. A 1979 nationwide survey showed that although marijuana use was still on the

128

rise, even young people were beginning to recognize the dangers of heavy use. Among young adults aged eighteen to twenty-five, 65.3 percent agreed that marijuana can cause decreased motivation in heavy users,[7] and an even higher proportion (72.2 percent) believed that marijuana intoxication impairs automobile driving performance.[8]

And, of course, crime is directly linked to drugs. Petty theft, shoplifting, burglary, muggings, and prostitution by users; robbery and shootings among dealers; and violence, hijacking, and smuggling by multi-million-dollar drug runners are all inevitable aspects of the drug scene.

Few thoughtful people deny the social costs of drug use and abuse. Yet many users deny that their use has any ill effects on them personally. To those of us who have studied drugs and the problems associated with drug use, the ill effects upon the individual and society are obvious: to take drugs is to take risks.

Footnotes

[1] Hardin B. Jones and Helen C. Jones, *Sensual Drugs* (New York: Cambridge University Press, 1977), p. 30.
[2] Samuel Irwin, *Drugs of Abuse* (Madison, WI: STASH, Inc., 1979), p. 26.
[3] Edward C. Farley, Yoav Santo, and David W. Speck, ''Multiple Drug-Abuse Patterns of Youths in Treatment,'' in *Youth Drug Abuse: Problems, Issues, and Treatment,* eds. George M. Beschner and Alfred S. Friedman (Lexington, MA: Lexington Books, 1979), p. 166.
[4] Jones and Jones, p. 65.
[5] Jones and Jones, p. 38.
[6] Jones and Jones, p. 37.
[7] National Institute on Drug Abuse, *National Survey on Drug Abuse: Main Findings 1979* (Washington, DC: Government Printing Office, 1980), p. 116, Table 73.
[8] National Institute on Drug Abuse, p. 118, Table 75.

129

10

A CATALOG OF PSYCHOACTIVE DRUGS

The following guide to psychoactive substances is designed to give parents essential information about the drugs their children may be using. Psychoactive drugs have been categorized in a variety of ways. We have kept our categories simple: drugs that activate the central nervous system (amphetamines, cocaine, hallucinogens, nicotine); drugs that depress the central nervous system (alcohol, sedatives, opiates); and drugs that produce multiple effects (marijuana, phencyclidine).

Amphetamines, cocaine, and hallucinogens are stimulants that intensify perceptions and awareness, sometimes disturbing the information-processing functions of the brain, even to the point of psychosis.

Alcohol, sedatives (sleeping pills and tranquilizers), inhalants, and opiates are depressants that produce the opposite effects. They enable the individual to withdraw from the world, sometimes to the point of coma and death.

And some drugs, like marijuana or phencyclidine (PCP or angel dust), produce both stimulant and depressant effects, often with unpredictable results.

The effects of all drugs vary greatly, depending on the *size* and *purity* of the dose, the *way it is taken* into the body, the *frequency* of use, the *social setting* in which it is used, and the *expectations* of the user. Furthermore, users often combine drugs in hopes of experiencing several effects at once. Multiple-substance use has become a common phenomenon among youths in all parts of the world. Surveys in the United States show that next to tobacco and alcohol, marijuana and alcohol are the two substances most regularly combined by adolescents, and the most prevalent three-drug combinations are alcohol-marijuana-hashish, followed by alcohol-marijuana-amphetamines, and alcohol-marijuana-inhalants. Numerous two-drug combinations by older drug users are marijuana-PCP, heroin-cocaine (the classic "speedball"), heroin-methamphetamine, and cocaine-methaqualone.

In addition, the effects of drugs purchased on the street are especially unpredictable because of the near certainty that they have been adulterated with other substances (some of which can be toxic) or that other substances have been substituted for the drugs the user believes he or she is buying.

Therefore, the descriptions that follow apply to the drugs in their pure state. However, even when they are pure, there can be wide variations in the effects that result.

DRUGS THAT ACTIVATE THE CENTRAL NERVOUS SYSTEM

DRUG TYPE: STIMULANTS

GENERIC NAMES	COMMON OR BRAND NAMES	SLANG NAMES
Amphetamine (methamphetamine)	Benzedrine, Biphetamine, Delcobese, Desoxyn, Dexedrine, Mediatric, Methedrine	beans, bennies, black beauties, black mollies, copilots, crank, crossroads, crystal, dexies, double

131

DRUG TYPE: STIMULANTS *(continued)*

GENERIC NAMES	COMMON OR BRAND NAMES	SLANG NAMES
		cross, hearts, meth, lid poppers, peaches, pep pills, roses, speed, thrusters, truck drivers, uppers
Amphetamine-Barbiturate combinations	Daprisal, Desbutal, Dexamyl, Tedral	Christmas trees, purple hearts, dexies
Caffeine	coffee, tea, cocoa, cola drinks, No-Doz, diet pills	
Cocaine	cocaine	blow, C, coca, coke, flake, girl, heaven dust, lady, leaf, nose candy, paradise, rock, snow, toot, uptown, white
Methylphenidate	Ritalin	
Nicotine	tobacco products (cigarettes, cigars, pipe tobacco, chewing tobacco, snuff)	
Phenmetrazine	Preludin, Endurets	
Phenylpropanolamine	Nonprescription diet pills, cough and cold remedies	

Effects

Stimulants dilate the pupils; increase perspiration, respiration, heart rate, and blood pressure; and cause trembling. They are popular because they produce high

132

energy, alertness, exhilaration, talkativeness, asser-
tiveness, confidence, and other pleasurable sensations. Because they also reduce appetite, they are an
ingredient in diet pills. In larger doses, they can create
an intense feeling of well-being (euphoria), and they
can enhance sexual pleasure by delaying orgasm.
When taken intravenously, amphetamines or cocaine
can bring on orgasmic experiences, known as
"flashes" or "rushes." Larger doses can also produce
irritability, restlessness, anxiety, and paranoia. Pro-
tracted use of stimulants is followed by a period of
depression, called crashing, which encourages re-
newed use of stimulants. Physical exertion can be dangerous, and fatalities have been reported among athletes using moderate amounts of stimulants during
extreme activity.

Risks

Users frequently develop a psychological dependence
on stimulants, and with chronic high doses, tolerance
and physical dependency have also been noted. Withdrawal symptoms for chronic users include severe
depression and intense craving for the drug, and are
often accompanied by extreme exhaustion. Chronic
high dosage frequently results in malnutrition and pre-
mature aging, and such users risk pneumonia, tuberculosis, and hepatitis from unsterile injection equipment. Aggressive behavior is common, and constant
heavy use can lead to psychotic behavior indistin-
guishable from paranoid schizophrenia; in severe
cases, delirium and hallucination can result. Bizarre
accidents and homicides are the occasional result of
amphetamine psychosis, usually brought on by a binge
of several days to a week of continuous injection (a
"speed run" by a "speed freak"). Cocaine psychosis

is often characterized by the belief that bugs are crawl-
ing under the skin and by visual hallucinations. With
chronic high doses of stimulants, there is also evidence of liver damage and brain-cell injury, and such
doses can result in convulsions, coma, cerebral hemorrhages, and death.

There is currently considerable controversy over
the hazards of phenylpropanolamine, the main ingredient in over-the-counter diet pills and some cough
and cold remedies. There are numerous reports of confusion, gross anxiety, extreme hypertension (high
blood pressure), strokes, and death resulting from cerebral hemorrhage, even with recommended dosages
of these nonprescription drug products. The nicotine
in tobacco plants is one of the most toxic drugs known,
and is considered a poison hazardous to health.

Remarks

The occasional use of stimulants like amphetamines
to remain alert or improve performance is common
practice among many, including such different types
as students, truck drivers, athletes, military personnel,
and others, and because of the exhilarating effects, it
is very easy to continue using them on an increasingly
regular basis. Cocaine is particularly seductive because of the intensity of its pleasurable effects, and its
use has expanded rapidly in the last few years. Often
erroneously thought to be free of unsafe side effects,
cocaine has a potential for extraordinary psychological
dependence. It is an extract from the leaves of the
coca plant found mainly in Peru and Bolivia, where
the leaves have long been chewed as a mild tonic.

Cocaine is extremely expensive. As one well-
known entertainer remarked, "Cocaine is nature's way
of telling you that you're making too much money."

Street cocaine is therefore commonly cut with a variety of substances: milk sugar, mannitol, and local anesthetics such as lidocaine. Cocaine's high price has made it a status symbol with high-paid athletes, entertainers, and others with affluence, but its use by adolescents in all income groups is increasing. Usually inhaled, cocaine is also smoked in a highly concentrated form known as free-base. Like amphetamines, cocaine produces intense short-term feelings of euphoria, high energy, and mental alertness.

Cocaine, amphetamine, and methamphetamine are also widely believed to be aphrodisiacs, and in addition to being injected or snorted up the nostrils, they are sometimes applied directly to the genitals. Stimulant users report intensified sexual feelings and marathon sexual activities. Cocaine is judged by users to be superior to the other stimulants in this respect. However, users also often report sexual arousal without climax.

Some individuals resort to depressants such as heroin, or to combined stimulant-depressants such as Dexamyl (Dexedrine and Amytal—"purple hearts") to counteract this and other effects of stimulants. Occasionally, because the level of sensual experience is so high with cocaine and amphetamines, young users become psychologically addicted after the first use.

DRUGS THAT ACTIVATE
THE CENTRAL NERVOUS SYSTEM

DRUG TYPE: **HALLUCINOGENS**

GENERIC NAMES	COMMON OR BRAND NAMES	SLANG NAMES
Datura Strammonium	Jimsonweed	
Ipomea Pupurea	Morning glory seeds	

DRUG TYPE: **HALLUCINOGENS** *(continued)*

GENERIC NAMES	COMMON OR BRAND NAMES	SLANG NAMES
Lysergic acid diethylamide	LSD, LSD-25, lysergide	acid, blotter acid, cubes, microdots, orange sunshine, paper acid, purple haze, sunshine, tabs, wedges, window panes
Mescaline	mescaline, peyote	buttons, cactus, mesc, mescal, mescal buttons
Myristica fragrans	nutmeg, mace	
Psilocybin	Mexican mushroom, Psilocybe mushroom, sacred mushroom	buttons, magic mushrooms
Synthetic Mescaline-Amphetamine compounds	DET DMT DOB DOM (STP) MDA MMDA	businessman's trip STP the love drug

Effects

Hallucinogens can cause dilated pupils, increased pulse and blood pressure, decreased or increased salivation, dizziness, tremors, nausea and vomiting (primarily with peyote). But hallucinogens have their main effect on perception: sight, sound, and touch become extraordinarily sensitive. Colors and sounds take on great brilliance and intensity, often in unique ways. Colors are "heard," music is "seen." Emotional reactions are intensified, time perceptions are distorted, and a loss of self-awareness (depersonalization) and

136

hallucinations can occur. The emotional outcome for the individual varies greatly; the same person can have different reactions on different occasions. Depending on personality, moods, companions, environmental setting, and the type, strength, and purity of the drug, reactions can range from intense panic to deep tranquility.

Hallucinogen users are often motivated by the hope of dramatic mystical experience in which deep personal or spiritual insights are achieved, or creative capacities are awakened, resulting in a changed outlook after the experience. Flashbacks—the recurrence of hallucinations and other drug effects days or months later—are frequently reported by heavy users. However, they do not seem to recur if a year has elapsed since the last use of hallucinogens or since the last flashback. A full-fledged LSD trip can last nine hours or longer.

Risks

Although a slight possibility for psychological dependence on hallucinogens exists, physical addiction does not seem to occur. However, tolerance to high doses quickly develops. There are no documented withdrawal symptoms, and fatalities are due to accidents resulting from bizarre behavior rather than drug effects. The main dangers of hallucinogen use are psychological. In the short term, extreme disorientation can result in intense anxiety and panic, paranoia, psychosis, and dangerously bizarre behavior. This seems to be particularly true for individuals who are already emotionally disturbed. Longer term hazards include continued psychotic episodes and depression, withdrawal from normal activities, loss of motivation, and the great anxiety that accompanies flashbacks.

Research indicates that heavy use of LSD causes changes in mental functions suggestive of organic brain damage, such as impaired memory and attention span, mental confusion, and difficulty with abstract thinking. In experiments on spiders under the influence of LSD, the spiders weave chaotic and incomplete webs, and the damage to their nervous system is permanent. Whether such mental changes are irreversible in chronic high-dose human users has not been conclusively demonstrated. A more immediate danger is the high likelihood that substances sold as hallucinogens are in reality contaminated by other more dangerous drugs.

Remarks

LSD is the most popular hallucinogen among young people, and because it is so easily manufactured, it is the most available. LSD is an extremely powerful drug, five thousand times as potent as mescaline, for example. Doses are measured in micrograms, and one ounce of LSD is equivalent to three hundred thousand doses. In its early use, it was often applied to sugar cubes by the user, but it is now sold in tablet form, thin squares of gelatin called window panes, and perforated sheets of blotter paper. Some enterprising manufacturers have printed Walt Disney characters or other cartoon favorites on each square of blotter acid. LSD seemed to have had its heyday during the "psychedelic" period of the 1960's, but surveys indicate it is making a comeback among a new generation of adolescents.

LSD is a synthetic drug. It and a number of synthetic variations of mescaline and amphetamine (such as DOM, also called STP) are manufactured in clandestine laboratories. Many other hallucinogens occur in a natural state and have long been an integral part of the religious and social life of native cultures. Peyote cactus, the sacred Psilocybe mushroom of Mexico, and Cohoba snuff of South America, are examples.

DRUGS THAT DEPRESS
THE CENTRAL NERVOUS SYSTEM

DRUG TYPE: **SEDATIVES**

GENERIC NAMES	COMMON OR BRAND NAMES	SLANG NAMES
BARBITURATES		
Amobarbital	Amytal	barbs, blues, blue
Amo/Secobarbital	Tuinal	devils
Pentobarbital	Nembutal	rainbows, tooies
		nemmies, yellows,
Phenobarbital	Luminal	yellow jackets
		goofballs, phennies,
Secobarbital	Seconal	purple hearts
		F-40's, reds, redbirds,
		red devils
NON-BARBITURATES		
Ethchlorvynol	Placidyl	dyls
Glutethimide	Doriden	D
Methaqualone	Quaalude, Sopor,	ludes, sopor, Q's,
	Parest, Optimil,	714's, vitamin Q,
	Somnifac, Mandrax,	heroin for lovers,
	Dimethacol,	wallbanger
	Biphetamine-T	
Methylprylon	Nodular	
TRANQUILIZERS		
Benzodiazepine	Valium, Librium,	downs, tranks
	Dalmane, Serax,	
	Tranxene, Clonopin	
Meprobamate	Miltown, Equanil,	
	Kesso-Bamate, SK-Bamate	
Mebutamate	Dormate	

139

Effects

Sedatives slow respiration, lower pulse and heart rate, produce dizziness, drowsiness, relaxation, loss of inhibition, talkativeness, slurred speech, difficulty in thinking, and alcohollike intoxication. Because sedatives depress the central nervous system, higher doses can produce muscular incoordination, staggering gait, stupor, sleep, unconsciousness, coma, and death. Commonly referred to as sleeping pills and tranquilizers, sedatives are used medically to induce sleep or to relieve anxiety and depression, and they are frequently overused for these reasons. Recreational users enjoy the feelings of intoxication, often accompanied by euphoria, that sedatives provide. The relaxation of inhibitions encourages sexual behavior and thus gives some of these drugs, most notably the extremely popular Quaalude, a reputation as aphrodisiacs. Impulsiveness, aggressiveness, and possible violence can also result from recreational use. Sedatives are also often taken in combination with other drugs such as alcohol, heroin, amphetamines, or cocaine, to offset the effects of stimulants or to create certain unusual effects. Use with alcohol is very common, and the combined depressant effects are more powerful than the user generally expects. The result is often accidental death.

Risks

Habituation, tolerance, and addiction are common problems for sedative users. Physical dependency can develop within two weeks of daily use. Common side effects include hangovers, skin rashes, nausea, weakness, and indigestion. Withdrawal symptoms are similar to delirium tremens of alcohol withdrawal, but more severe. They include restlessness, shaking, weakness, insomnia, abdominal cramps, nausea, vomiting, stomach hemorrhages, delirium, delusions, and convulsions. These symptoms are also more severe than those of heroin withdrawal and can be fatal if use is abruptly halted. With barbiturates in particular, tolerance develops rapidly, and the difference between a lethal dose and an effective dose becomes quite small. Barbiturates seem to be the drugs of choice for suicides; they are involved in nearly one-third of all reported drug-induced deaths.

"Luding out" with methaqualone (Quaalude, Sopor, etc.) is popularly believed to be a safe way to get high. However, methaqualone is no safer than barbiturates. Neither are the other non-barbiturates or the tranquilizers. They all produce tolerance, dependence, and life-threatening withdrawal illness, and death can result from overdose, withdrawal convulsions, or from combinations such as alcohol-methaqualone. The combined effects of less-than-lethal doses of alcohol and sedatives taken together can be deadly. The benzodiazepines (Valium, Librium, etc.) can also be addicting, but they seldom kill by themselves.

Remarks

Sedatives are abused by all age groups. Among the barbiturates most frequently used for recreation are those whose effects are of short duration such as secobarbital (Seconal) and pentobarbital (Nembutal). As with all psychoactive drugs, their effect depends on the expectations of the user. In a party atmosphere, barbiturates provide intoxication and excitement rather than sleep. Secobarbital is sometimes associated with aggressive behavior because of its disinhibiting effect.

Barbiturate addiction is medically more serious

than narcotic addiction. Death may occur if a barbiturate addict goes "cold turkey" and abruptly halts his or her use. Treatment generally involves substituting a long-acting barbiturate and then slowly withdrawing it under medical supervision.

Among the non-barbiturates, methaqualone is very popular with adolescent users, partially because it intoxicates without so much drowsiness as barbiturates. Because it loosens inhibitions, methaqualone also has a reputation as an aphrodisiac, although users sometimes state that sexual performance is impaired. Perhaps for this reason, a favorite combination of more adventurous users is "ludes and coke"—methaqualone and cocaine. For years, the high abuse potential of methaqualone went unrecognized, and many physicians prescribed it as safe and nonaddictive. Many users today still mistakenly believe the same thing.

DRUGS THAT DEPRESS
THE CENTRAL NERVOUS SYSTEM

DRUG TYPE: NARCOTICS

GENERIC NAMES	COMMON OR BRAND NAMES	SLANG NAMES
Codeine	pain relievers (Empirin with Codeine), cough syrups (Robitussin AC)	schoolboy
Heroin	heroin	boy, brown, brown sugar, caballo, chiva, crap, downtown, H, hombre, horse, junk, mexican mud, scag, shit, smack, stuff
Hydromorphone	Dilaudid	little D

142

DRUG TYPE: **NARCOTICS** *(continued)*

GENERIC NAMES	COMMON OR BRAND NAMES	SLANG NAMES
Meperidine (pethidine)	Demerol, Pethadol	demmies
Methadone	Dolophine, Methadose	meth, dollies
Morphine	morphine	cube, first line, goma, M, morph, morphy, mud
Opium	opium, Dover's powder, Paregoric, Parapectolin	blue velvet, black
Oxycodone	Percodan	perkies
Pentazocine	Talwin	T's
Propoxyphene	Davron, Darvon N	

Effects

The physiological effects of *narcotics* include slowing of respiration and heartbeat, lowering of body temperature, flushing of the skin, heaviness of the limbs, feelings of warmth in the abdomen, yawning, drowsiness ("nodding off"), dilation of the blood vessels with accompanying itching and sweating, constriction of the pupils, dizziness, skin rashes, constipation, nausea, and occasional vomiting (though vomiting is rare when tolerance is established). Psychological effects center around the euphoric and pain-relieving qualities of narcotics. Because of their analgesic effects, narcotics raise the threshold of pain and dramatically relieve the awareness of pain, discomfort, worry, and anxiety. Mental and physical perform-

143

ances are impaired; hunger and sex drives are reduced, a kind of mental clouding and inability to concentrate occurs, although occasionally stimulation and excitation can accompany use.

Upon injection, narcotics can also produce a "rush," a kind of sexual pleasure, often defined as a whole-body orgasm radiating from a warm feeling in the abdomen, although some users experience unpleasant sensations. It is the extreme euphoria, however, that makes narcotics such as heroin so appealing and dangerous. Euphoria—bodily comfort, a sense of well-being, absence of pain or stress, and a sense of emotional detachment—is the classic "high" of narcotics.

Risks

Narcotics are physically and psychologically addictive, and dependence can develop within weeks of regular use. Tolerance also develops, requiring larger and larger doses to achieve the desired effects. Addicts soon reach a point where euphoria is secondary to the need to avoid the pain of withdrawal symptoms and to maintain a "normal" state—that is, a satisfactory "nod."

Withdrawal symptoms are generally a reversal of the depressant effects on the central nervous system and include yawning, runny nose, sneezing, tearing of the eyes, increased salivation, sweating, chills, hot flushes, gooseflesh, nausea and vomiting, diarrhea, muscle and abdominal cramping, muscle spasms (the origin of the phrase "kicking the habit"), generalized body and bone aches, increased respiration, heart rate, and blood pressure, dehydration, loss of body weight, insomnia, anxiety, restlessness, nervousness, and irritability. Withdrawal symptoms can occur within three hours of the last dose, can reach a peak within thirty-six to seventy-two hours, and can last as long as ten days.

Withdrawal is rarely life-threatening, and "cold turkey" abstinence is the most effective means of detoxification. Although this process can be extremely painful, just how painful depends upon how large the habit is. Occasional users, "chippers" or "weekend warriors," show only mild symptoms—a runny nose, sneezing, tearing of the eyes, very like symptoms of the common cold. Users with a small daily habit have withdrawal symptoms resembling a very bad case of flu that lasts a few days. Most ex-addicts also report an intense craving for the drug, similar to hunger cravings but many times stronger, that can last for years. This makes narcotic addiction particularly difficult to overcome. During the beginning stages of use, there is danger of accidental death from overdose. Infants in the womb can become addicted and will suffer withdrawal symptoms upon birth.

Provided an addict can maintain a carefully controlled and relatively pure dosage, there are apparently few negative physiological effects of narcotic addiction. A surprising number of physicians and other biomedical workers are secret addicts who work in a normal fashion for years. Physicians have a high heroin-addiction rate compared to the general population. Although narcotics in pure form appear to cause much less permanent damage to the body than some drugs such as alcohol, tobacco, or amphetamines, other associated risks make narcotics very dangerous. Infection from unsterile needles can cause serum hepatitis, endocardic infection, abscesses, and tetanus. Death most often results from an overdose of the unknown substances with which street heroin is cut, or from lethal combinations with other drugs. Malnutrition and

145

high risk of accidental injury and violent death are consequences of the addict's life-style, as is punishment for criminal activities undertaken to support an expensive habit. An addict is likely to suffer from long-term emotional depression and loneliness, loss of sexual desire and capacity, and a deep-seated self-hatred caused by the inability to resist the intense craving for the drug. As one addict expressed it, heroin "has all the advantages of death, without its permanence."

Remarks

Narcotics are either opiates derived from the opium poppy *(Papaver somniferum)* or synthetic products that act like opiates. Morphine is the major active ingredient of opium and is widely used to alleviate pain, especially in terminally ill patients. Heroin is an illicit derivative of morphine, two to three times as powerful. Methadone is a synthetic narcotic used with varying success as a substitute for heroin in maintenance-therapy programs for heroin addicts. Heroin, methadone, codeine, Demerol, Dilaudid, and other narcotics are used interchangeably by addicts. The effects of all narcotics are roughly similar, but heroin is generally preferred, partly for its strength and partly because it is much less bulky than raw opium or refined morphine and therefore more suitable for smuggling.

A white powder, heroin is usually cut with milk sugar (for bulk), mannitol (a mild laxative to counteract the constipation that accompanies opiate use), and quinine (originally added to protect against malaria from dirty needles and retained because of its bitter taste, imitative of the taste of good heroin). However, other substances such as strychnine, flour,

146

cornstarch, talc, procaine and other local anesthetic agents are also used for cutting.

Some of these cause most of the deaths attributed to heroin "overdose." Because of adulterants, most street heroin is only about three percent pure, although recent supplies from the Middle East are extremely pure, ninety percent or more, and have killed unsuspecting users. Heroin is generally injected, either subcutaneously ("skin-popping"), or intravenously ("mainlining"), although very pure heroin can be smoked or snorted like cocaine.

Heroin is the least-used psychoactive substance— no doubt due as much to its high price as to its welldeserved reputation as a dangerous drug. Its use among adolescents is relatively limited compared to other drugs. In a national survey conducted in 1980, only 1.1 percent of high-school seniors reported using heroin, compared to 16 percent who acknowledged using cocaine and 60 percent who acknowledged using marijuana. But heroin use increases in the eighteen to twenty-five age group as sophistication and daring increase. Drug experts agree that the addiction potential of opiates is gravely underestimated, particularly by adolescent users. Although it was once thought that only certain personality types could become addicted, it now appears that almost anyone can get hooked on opiates under the right conditions of stress and access to narcotics. For example, many stable persons have become addicted to morphine in the course of a painful illness.

But heroin use does not automatically mean full-scale addiction. Some users maintain an "ice-cream habit": they are occasional users on weekends or at parties. It is estimated that there are two to three times as many "chippers" or "weekend warriors" as there are hard-core addicts (who number some 500,000 in

147

the United States—109,000 in the New York City area alone). Recent studies suggest there are people who can exercise some control over their heroin use, including some highly distinguished people who have had brilliant careers in spite of their addiction. And recently, heroin has become a status symbol for occasional users caught up in an affluent life-style. Heroin, like cocaine, is seen as exciting and glamorous, and can be obtained without the risks of a hustling street junkie. "When I want to get it," one New Yorker comments, "I can do it by the telephone. I can write a check. I can put it on my Mastercharge. How? There are certain restaurants, discos, and nightspots where it can turn up on the credit card as two bottles of Château Latour."[1]

However, to keep such recreational use within bounds appears to require not only regular access to heroin of high purity but considerable strength of character as well. In addition, much depends upon the social context in which heroin is used and upon the degree of the individual's self-esteem. The risk is very high that a chipper who believes he can't get hooked will soon find himself compulsively using heroin.

DRUGS THAT DEPRESS THE CENTRAL NERVOUS SYSTEM

DRUG TYPE: INHALANTS

Inhalants are chemical substances that evaporate upon exposure to the air, and can be thus drawn into the lungs. Most inhalants used for their psychoactive effects are commercial preparations designed for industrial, household, or medical uses. They include many solvents, nearly all aerosol sprays, some anesthetics, and the vasodilators amyl nitrite and butyl nitrite. Most of these are complex chemical compounds, classified variously by chemical groups such as hydrocarbons, aromatic hydrocarbons, aliphatic hydrocarbons, fluorocarbons, chlorinated hydrocarbons, aliphatic nitrites, alcohols, ketones, and esters. In addition, the formulations of many of these products are not chemically pure, and they often contain additives, such as lead in gasoline, that are more poisonous than the volatile substance itself.

Examples

Solvents	antifreeze, gasoline, nail polish and nail-polish remover, model cement, rubber cement, plastic cement, cleaning fluid, spot remover, dry cleaner, lighter fluid, charcoal-lighter fluid, paint, lacquer, enamel, varnish, paint and lacquer thinner, transmission fluid
Aerosols	spray paint, hair spray, insecticide, furniture polish, window cleaner, deodorant and antiperspirant, spray shoe polish, air sanitizers, and practically anything in a spray can
Anesthetics	nitrous oxide ("laughing gas," whipped cream propellant), Freon (refrigerants, aerosol propellants)
Vasodilators	amyl nitrite (medication for angina pectoris, room deodorizers, "snappers" and "poppers"), butyl nitrite

Effects

Depending on the size of the dose, the effects of inhaled volatile substances can range from mild intoxication to complete unconsciousness. The effects are immediate and may last from a few minutes to a few

149

hours, followed by drowsiness, occasional headache, nausea, and more rarely partial or total amnesia for the intoxicated period. The sought-after effects include dizziness, a sense of floating, giddiness, exhilaration and intense feelings of well-being, a loss of inhibitions resulting in reckless and impulsive behavior, a feeling of greatly increased power, distortions of space and visual perception, visual and auditory hallucinations. When inhaled, amyl nitrite and butyl nitrite expand the arteries and lower blood pressure; time seems to slow down, and this accounts for the sensation of prolonged orgasm that has made these substances popular.

Risks

Partial tolerance can develop with daily inhaling, and psychological dependence can develop with chronic use. The toxic effects of snorting are varied. Occasional use of inhalants is generally believed to result in no permanent damage, but numerous reports suggest that even first-time use may pose a threat to health. The greatest danger of inhalants is that there is almost always more than one toxic substance present, resulting in a more toxic net effect. Little is known about how single solvents damage organs, and less is known about the pharmacological action of a mixture of several volatile substances. This problem is further complicated when users combine inhalants with other depressants, such as alcohol.

Fluorocarbons (Freons) in aerosol sprays cause numerous deaths due to heart failure or inability to breathe due to freezing of the larynx. Permanent brain damage and death due to bone marrow problems and to liver, kidney, and other organ failures can result from chronic use of compounds containing hydro-

MARIJUANA

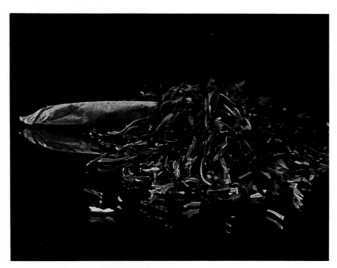

Top: Cannabis sativa, Marijuana (pot, weed, dope, grass) in joint form as it is prepared for smoking. Left: Cannabis plant. The flower clusters and top leaves contain a resin in which most of the THC is concentrated.

STIMULANTS

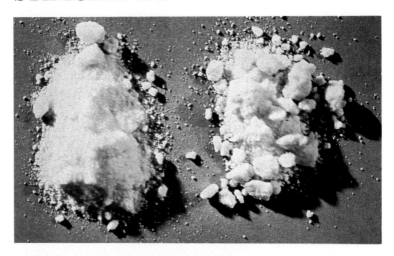

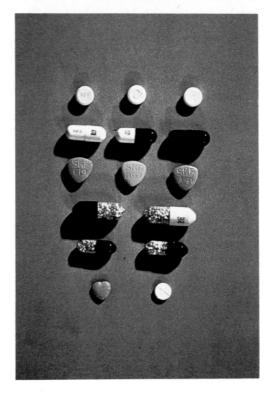

Top: Cocaine (snow, toot, coke) crystal and powder. Bottom: Methamphetamines (speed, bennies, meth) pills and capsules.

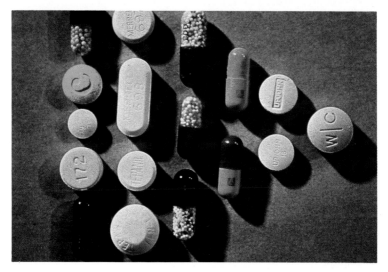

Top: Cocaine pa-
raphernalia.
Bottom: Anorec-
tic drugs (diet
pills).

NARCOTICS

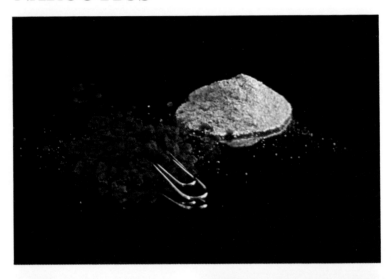

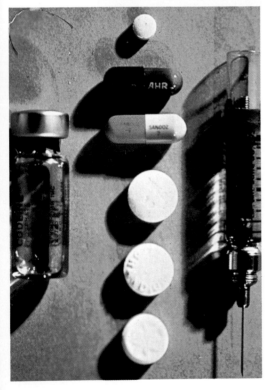

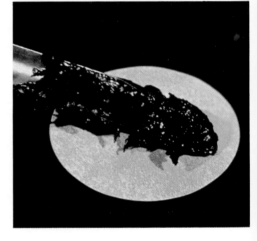

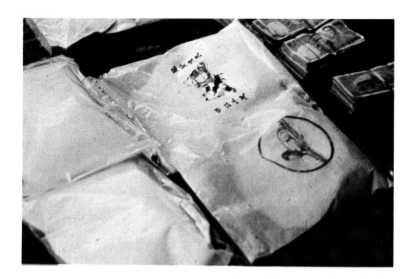

Top left: Heroin (smack, junk, horse) in pow-
der and crystal form.Top right:Heroin packed
in airtight plastic bags for shipping. Bottom
left: Codeine (schoolboy) pills, capsules, and
serum for injecting. Center: Opium gum (blue
velvet, black). Bottom right: Phencyclidine
(PCP, Angel Dust) once a legal anesthetic,
realized to be extremely dangerous.

SEDATIVES

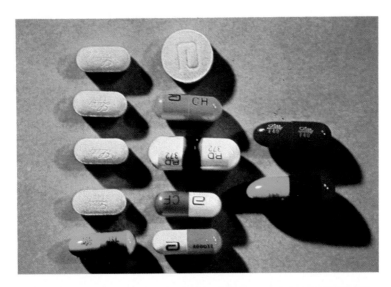

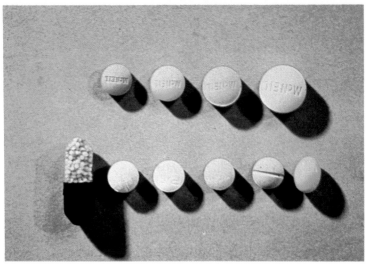

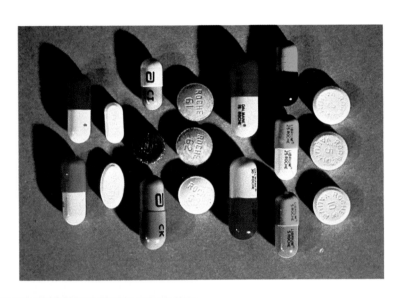

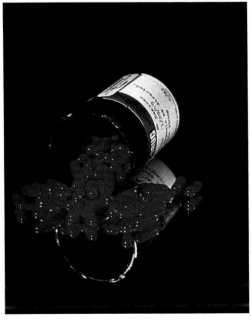

Top right: Barbiturates (Amobarbital, Pentobarbital). Top left: Benzodizaphine (tranquilizers, downs, tranks). Bottom left: Phenobarbital (goofballs, phennies, purple hearts). Bottom right: Secobarbital (F-40's, reds, redbirds).

HALLUCINOGENS

Top: Peyote Cactus (mesc, cactus). Right: Psilocybin Mushroom (buttons, magic mushroom).

carbons. Hydrocarbons are contained in gasoline, benzene (present in gasoline, rubber cement, tube repair kits, cleaning fluid, and numerous other products), carbon tetrachloride (spot remover), n-hexane (airplane glue), paint and paint thinner, adhesives, degreasers, and other products. Numerous deaths are attributed to suffocation from inhaling substances in a tightly closed space or with a plastic bag over the head, and accidental injury or death results from impaired judgment and reckless actions.

The chief danger of nitrous oxide appears to be the possibility of stupor, coma, brain damage, or death from oxygen deprivation produced by sustained inhalation of the gas. Little is yet known about the long-term effects of amyl nitrite other than the known side effects of occasional headache, nausea, vomiting, flushing of the face, and temporary visual disorders.

Remarks

Solvent and aerosol sniffing is predominant among elementary schoolchildren and young adolescents, most likely because aerosols, paint cans, gasoline, nail polish, and the like are readily available, inexpensive, legal, compactly packaged, and quick acting. The fumes of these substances are most often inhaled from a rag or a plastic bag into which the substance has been poured or sprayed. Users may be classified as either experimental or chronic. Experimental use is widespread among schoolchildren and is regarded by some as part of a normal adolescent curiosity. Chronic inhalant abusers often have unstable family backgrounds. Inhalant abuse is an international phenomenon; epidemics have broken out in Japan, Europe, and elsewhere. The publicity surrounding the discovery in the early 1960's of a few children sniffing glue in

Denver is now regarded as having been a major factor in the spread of the problem to other cities. This incident is often cited as an example of how exaggerated concern and misleading information help create a problem. The widely broadcast news accounts gave curious children elsewhere explicit instructions, and hysterical warnings by misinformed adults were met by skepticism.

Recently, amyl nitrite has become popular as an inhaled substance that prolongs orgasm. A 1980 federal study of high-school seniors indicated that amyl and butyl nitrite inhalants had been tried by one of every nine seniors (eleven percent). Originally prescribed for the chest pains of heart trouble, amyl nitrite was packaged in small cloth-encased ampules that could be crushed in the hand and the fumes inhaled, hence the names snappers or poppers. But now small bottles of amyl or butyl nitrite are available in adult bookstores allegedly for use as room deodorizers. They are labeled with exotic names: Rip, Kick, Locker Room, Rush, Bullet, Jac Aroma, and Aroma of Men.

DRUGS THAT DEPRESS
THE CENTRAL NERVOUS SYSTEM

DRUG TYPE: **ALCOHOL**

Ethyl alcohol, or ethanol, is the active principle of beer, wine, and distilled liquor. It is a natural substance produced by the fermenting of sugars in grapes, grains, berries, or molasses. In the United States, the alcohol content of distilled liquor is expressed as "proof." The proof rating is equal to twice the actual alcohol content by volume (for example, 86 proof equals 43 percent alcohol). Ethanol is chemically similar to ether and has similar anesthetic properties, but it is not to be confused with methanol (wood alcohol, a component of antifreeze compounds and some fuels), or isopropyl alcohol (rubbing alcohol), both of which are toxic and can be fatal if consumed. Wine, beer, ale, and distilled-alcohol products ("hard liquors") have been used worldwide for centuries for social, medical, and religious purposes.

Effects

Alcohol is a depressant whose well-known effects vary depending on the amount imbibed, the rate of absorption into the bloodstream, the rate of metabolism by the liver, the drinker's level of tolerance, the drinker's personality, and the social setting. Since alcohol requires no digestion, it passes directly into the bloodstream, although food in the stomach can slow down the rate of absorption. In small doses, and among convivial company, alcohol usually produces a relaxing effect. Because it lowers inhibitions, as all depressants do, alcohol's first effects are often stimulantlike—producing an increase in talkativeness and amiability, and occasional aggressiveness or amorousness. With greater doses, the effects of sedation appear: slurred speech, incoordination, staggering gait, impaired thinking and judgment, memory loss and blackouts, emotional instability and belligerence, and loss of sexual ability. Very high doses can result in unconsciousness, coma, and death from respiratory and heart failure. If more alcohol is drunk than can be metabolized by the body, the alcohol accumulates in the blood. Blood alcohol concentration (BAC) is expressed in percentages. In most states, a person is legally intoxicated with a BAC of 0.10 percent, the equivalent of three to four drinks or three to four beers drunk within one hour by a 160-pound person.

Risks

It is possible to be a moderate social drinker without incurring serious health risks, although some recent studies indicate that the amounts of alcohol consumed by many "social drinkers" are sufficient to cause liver damage without ever having been drunk. However, millions of people are risking their health through immoderate drinking. Alcohol is considered by many to be the most dangerous psychoactive substance known to man, and yet it is more often thought of as a beverage than as a drug. Alcohol addiction is marked by both psychological and physical dependence, and tolerance is developed in the habitual drinker. Withdrawal symptoms range in severity from hangover with its upset stomach, headache, thirst, and fatigue, to tremors, nausea, anxiety, perspiration, cramps, vomiting, and, in cases of extreme addiction, frightening hallucinations, convulsions, delirium, and possible death from respiratory or heart failure. The extreme stage of withdrawal, known as delirium tremens, has an eight percent fatality rate.

Heavy users also risk the lowered resistance to disease that results from an inadequate diet. Cirrhosis of the liver and other gastrointestinal disorders, heart disease, oral cancer, skin diseases, loss of brain cells, and neurologic and psychiatric diseases are a few of the many alcohol-related disorders that can accompany abuse. Heavy drinkers cut their life expectancy by about ten years. The latest studies of the condition known as fetal alcohol syndrome indicate that serious damage to the unborn child can occur as early as three weeks into the pregnancy, which is long before most women realize they are pregnant. Although chronic alcohol use has been the usual focus of research into this syndrome, recent evidence suggests that even one or two bouts of heavy drinking early in the pregnancy

154

can injure the fetus. Fetal alcohol syndrome annually affects between 1 in 300 and 1 in 750 births in the United States and takes the form of retarded growth, facial deformities, mental retardation, defects in the central nervous system, or stillbirth.

Alcohol can be extremely hazardous when combined with other drugs, particularly sedatives. This is due to a phenomenon known as potentiation, in which the effects of one or both drugs are unanticipatedly increased. For example, when marijuana and alcohol are used together, the normal reflex that causes the body to expel excessive alcohol by vomiting is suppressed by marijuana, and injury and death can result from alcohol poisoning.

Excessive alcohol use also affects the entire social system. More than half of all traffic fatalities involve drinking drivers, and this percentage is much higher among young people. Annually some twenty-five thousand people die and hundreds of thousands are injured in accidents involving excessive alcohol use. It is estimated that some ninety percent of all assaults and fifty to sixty percent of all murders are committed by persons while under the influence of alcohol. Other police statistics on robbery, rape, battered wives and children, and suicide reflect a strong connection with excessive alcohol consumption.

Remarks

Over sixty percent of the population of America are regular users of alcohol. Of this number, it is estimated that some ten million are alcoholics, and, according to recent government estimates, three million of these are teenagers. A 1978 survey of high-school students showed that seventy percent had tried alcohol by the tenth grade. Other studies indicate that over fifty percent of all adolescents drink at least once a month; and, in a 1980 study of high-school seniors, forty-one percent reported that they had engaged in heavy drinking (defined as a minimum of four to five drinks) at least every other weekend.

Alcoholism may be defined as the use of alcoholic beverages to such an extent that bodily or mental health is adversely affected and normal personal, social, and occupational behaviors are disrupted. Alcoholism may take the form of heavy steady drinking or of occasional bouts of intense drinking. Early warning signs include alteration of personality when drinking, drinking to escape problems, preoccupation with drinking, guilt feelings about drinking, sneaking drinks, and difficulty in stopping drinking. Blackouts (temporary losses of memory) are a definite sign of developing alcoholism. While there is no way to predict who will be an alcoholic, alcoholics tend to have certain personality characteristics in common, such as feelings of inadequacy and inability to tolerate frustration. Many alcoholics exhibit symptoms of serious mental illness, and nearly half are either products of broken homes or have at least one alcoholic parent. There is some evidence that a tendency toward alcoholism may be inherited. And certain cultural groups (such as some northern Europeans) and tribal peoples whose cultural life and social system have been disrupted (such as Eskimos and North American Indians) seem to be more susceptible to alcoholism than others.

DRUGS WITH MULTIPLE EFFECTS ON THE CENTRAL NERVOUS SYSTEM

DRUG TYPE: MARIJUANA

Marijuana (grass, pot, dope, smoke, gauge, weed) is the air-dried, shredded leaves, stems, and flowering tops of the hemp plant, *Cannabis sativa*. Its use as a psychoactive substance spread westward from ancient China to India, North Africa, Europe, and then to North and South America. As hemp, the plant has been a major crop in many parts of the world, used for food, oil, and medicine, but primarily as a supply of fiber for rope, sails, and fabric. Although marijuana contains numerous chemicals, its principal psychoactive component is delta-9-tetrahydrocannabinol (THC). Delta-9-THC is one of a unique group of chemicals called cannabinoids found only in the cannabis plant. The flower clusters and top leaves of the plant contain a resin in which most of the THC is concentrated. Cannabis grows in many parts of the world, and marijuana prepared from it varies in potency depending on climate, soil conditions, methods of cultivation, time of harvesting, and means of preparation. In addition, some strains of cannabis contain more THC than others. Specialized cultivation can also increase the THC content. For example, because unfertilized female cannabis plants produce more resin, weeding out the male plants produces a high-potency marijuana known as sinsemilla (Spanish for "seedless"). Over the past decade, competition for lucrative marijuana profits, and more sophisticated growing techniques have produced marijuana with higher THC content. Today the average THC content of marijuana is about four percent; sinsemilla may contain as much as seven percent.

Hashish (hash, herb) is an extract of the cannibis resin, typically containing five to ten times as much THC as marijuana. Consolidated into a solid form, hashish's strength is judged by how dark it is. Deep cocoa brown or black indicates high potency. Hash oil (superpot, honey) is a refined form of the resin with a very high concentration of THC—from twenty percent to ninety percent. THC itself has been synthesized in the laboratory, but synthetic THC is chemically unstable and so far very difficult to produce. Thus it is very likely that anything sold on the street as THC is something else, such as LSD or PCP or some other questionable mixture.

Marijuana is generally smoked in cigarettes (called joints), in pipes, or through a variety of filtering pipes called bongs. Heat accelerates the activity of delta-9-THC. Although marijuana may be eaten—for example, baked in cookies or brownies—smoking allows greater control of the amount of the dose. Hashish may be eaten or smoked; a drop or two of hash oil may be added to a joint or to a regular cigarette.

Effects

Marijuana is a unique psychoactive substance not only because of its chemical composition but also because of the variety of effects it can produce. Sometimes classified as a hallucinogen, marijuana is both a stimulant and a depressant. In addition, its effects depend not only upon the THC content but upon the experience and expectations of the user. Thus, any description can only indicate the general range of effects users may experience.

Physiological symptoms of marijuana use include reddening of the eyes and facial skin, increase in heart rate, dizziness, a buzzing in the ears, and dry mouth. Sometimes nausea, vomiting, and diarrhea are experienced by beginning users. As with many other psychoactive drugs, marijuana's effects must often be interpreted as pleasurable before they can be enjoyed. Many inexperienced users are frightened by marijuana's disorienting effects and react with panic, while other first-time users may merely feel fatigued and depressed.

Normally, however, low doses of marijuana give the user a mild sense of intoxication, along with a sense of well-being. Hunger, especially for sweets, is often experienced. Words and phrases, or the actions of others, seem indescribably funny. Talkativeness and gaiety are followed by feelings of calm, relaxation, and goodwill toward oneself and others, a state sometimes referred to as being "mellowed out." Experienced users are able to suppress the effect of low doses, so that an observer may not be aware that the user is high.

Higher doses can bring on a feeling of heightened awareness and increased sensory perception (sounds, colors, taste, and touch are intensified), spatial distortions (objects at a distance seem closer), temporal distortions (an elapsed minute seems much longer), and clouded thought processes (things just thought, said, or seen are forgotten, and gaps occur in the flow of thoughts). Emotions may fluctuate rapidly because of fragmented thoughts and associations that accompany shifting sensory imagery. Stronger doses intensify these reactions and can induce hallucinations, distorted perceptions of one's body, a sense of depersonalization or of being outside of one's self, expansive feelings of self-importance, a sense of mystical insight into the meaning of life, or feelings of fear, anxiety, and panic. Because of its disinhibiting effects, marijuana is often associated by users with enhanced sexual pleasure.

The effects of smoking marijuana are generally felt within minutes, reach a high point within half an hour, and diminish within two or three hours. Headache is a frequently mentioned aftereffect.

An unusual effect of marijuana—known as a contact high—occasionally affects some nonusers who become mildly stoned when in proximity to marijuana smokers. This is generally thought to be a sympathetic response by highly suggestible individuals, although one study indicates that passive inhalation of marijuana smoke is the physiological basis for this effect.

Risks

There is little evidence of physical dependency or withdrawal symptoms, but psychological dependency can develop in habitual users of marijuana. A slight tolerance appears to develop with heavy use but not with moderate use. Death from overdose is unknown. The most common adverse reaction to higher doses of marijuana is a bad trip—acute anxiety and panic.

There is convincing scientific evidence that marijuana interferes with short-term memory, intellectual functions, and psychomotor skills. Driving, flying, and other activities requiring concentration and complex psychomotor skills are thus hazardous while using marijuana. This conclusion is reinforced by several state studies of traffic accidents and by the findings of the most recent National Survey on Drug Abuse, conducted by the National Institute on Drug Abuse, which report that a substantial majority of young adults ages eighteen to twenty-five and older adults believe that "getting really high [on marijuana] shortly before driving would cause a person to drive less well than he or she usually does."

There is strong evidence that marijuana smoking has adverse effects on the respiratory system, effects similar to the irritation caused by tobacco smoke. Habitual users can suffer chronic sore throat, laryngitis, and pharyngitis. Chronic bronchitis, asthma, and emphysema are associated with heavy, long-term marijuana use. Although studies indicate that marijuana smoke contains more coal tars and other carcinogens than tobacco smoke, as yet there is no direct evidence

160

linking marijuana with lung cancer in humans. Based on the accumulated findings of clinical and experimental evidence, however, there is a strong likelihood that daily marijuana smoking may lead to lung damage similar to the effects of heavy cigarette smoking, and the likelihood is even greater for those who smoke both marijuana and tobacco. Surveys indicate that many marijuana users are multiple substance users. There is some evidence that marijuana intensifies the effects of other drugs and that it can be potentially toxic or fatal when combined with alcohol, caffeine, sedatives, or amphetamines.

The evidence of risk is less clear cut for other potential medical hazards, such as the possibility that marijuana causes brain atrophy, cell damage, chromosome damage, reduced levels of the hormone testosterone, lowered sperm count, and damage to the body's immune system. At present, research findings on these subjects are divided, and any long-term significance has yet to be determined. Until conclusive results are established, these effects must be regarded only as possible hazards.

It has been demonstrated that the active principle of marijuana, delta-9-tetrahydrocannabinol (THC), remains in the body for long periods of time, although potential implications of this finding have yet to be definitively proved. Using radioactively tagged THC, researchers have found that delta-9-THC accumulates in the fatty tissues of the body and in the brain, with significant amounts still present many days after cessation of use, and trace amounts are detectable after thirty to sixty days. This THC residue may account for the absence of marijuana withdrawal symptoms.

The particular risks for women are not yet well established, but whatever risk marijuana presents for women is also a risk for fetuses and nursing babies.

161

Animal studies have shown that THC and other chemicals in marijuana accumulate in the placenta and embryonic material and are present in breast milk up to four hours after smoking.

Chronic use of marijuana has been associated with the "amotivational syndrome"—that is, a loss of interest in all activities except those related to drug use. The amotivational syndrome appears to be the result of subtle personality changes characterized by apathy, lack of ambition and motivation, short attention span, poor judgment, fragmented thinking, introversion, loss of insight, unrealistic or magical ideas, and an inability to conceive or carry out complex plans or realistic preparations for the future. The fact that such a syndrome appears in long-term heavy users of cannabis is incontrovertible; it has been noted among the hashish users of India, North Africa, and the Middle East as well as among the "potheads," "airheads," and "space cadets" of America. The question is whether marijuana use is responsible for such behavior, or whether such individuals were predisposed to a pattern of discouragement and dropping out that included marijuana use. It has been pointed out that lack of motivation can also be found in those who overuse alcohol, sedatives, or narcotics. But regardless of its origin, the link between marijuana and low motivation is well known and well-understood by marijuana users themselves. For example, the 1979 National Survey on Drug Abuse reported that "30% of the young adults [18–25] and about 25% of the older persons who have used marijuana on at least 100 occasions report that at one time *they themselves stopped caring and did not try as hard* because of steady or daily marijuana use. . . . Overall, about half of the young adults who have used marijuana at least 100 times—and a clear majority of all other groups—

believe that steady marijuana use would cause 'a hard-working person to stop caring and not try as hard.' ''

The occurrence of the amotivational syndrome among adolescents who use marijuana daily is, in our opinion, one of the chief risks associated with marijuana or any other drug used regularly by adolescents. The teenage years are a time for growth and development of coping skills, and habitual marijuana use can interfere with the acquisition of the skills, attitudes, and experiences necessary for emotional maturity.

Remarks

Marijuana is the third most commonly used psychoactive substance after alcohol and tobacco. Recent survey figures (1979) indicate that over fifty-four million Americans—more than twenty-five percent of the population—have tried marijuana at least once. Use is highest among young adults ages eighteen to twenty-five; sixty-eight percent report having tried it. Of the twelve to seventeen age group, thirty-one percent acknowledged use on at least one occasion. As children grow up, their chances of becoming daily users increase; one in twenty-five adolescents ages twelve to seventeen reported themselves daily users; among sixteen- to seventeen-year-olds, one in eleven are daily users; and the figure for youths eighteen to twenty-five years old is one in nine. Reported marijuana use has been increasing by substantial amounts every year since the early sixties up until 1982, when national survey figures showed a small but significant decline.

Advanced cultivation methods and sophisticated smuggling techniques have made marijuana production and sales a growth industry, accounting for about thirty-five percent of the illicit drug market. There are plantations in South America, Mexico, Southeast Asia, the Middle East, and elsewhere; and sinsemilla cultivation in California, Oregon, and Hawaii is an agrobusiness with annual profits estimated at nearly $200 million. ''Head shops'' are a related industry. Retailers and wholesalers of smoking paraphernalia legally sell millions of dollars' worth of cigarette papers, roach clips (used to hold the small burning end of a joint), bongs and pipes in great variety (water pipes, air-driven pipes, ice pipes or chillers), growing kits, separation gins and sifters (to clean and refine marijuana), camouflaged ''stash'' containers, books and magazines of instruction, commentary, and advice as well as paraphernalia designed for use with other illicit substances, such as cocaine spoons, scales and balances, diluents and adulterants used to cut drugs, processing and testing equipment, capsules, envelopes and other packaging containers, and hypodermic syringes and equipment.

There are medical uses for marijuana and THC that currently being investigated. Marijuana has been used therapeutically since ancient times as a cure for numerous ailments such as toothache, dysmenorrhea, and rheumatism. Under federally monitored research, marijuana has shown some effectiveness in the treatment of glaucoma by reducing intra-ocular pressure; in the control of nausea, vomiting, and loss of appetite following chemotherapy treatments for cancer; in the relief of the muscle spasms of cerebral palsy, multiple sclerosis, and certain kinds of strokes; as an anticonvulsant in persons with epilepsy; and as a bronchial dilator for asthma victims. However, its usefulness has so far been judged to be limited because of numerous undesirable side effects, because of the possibility of developing tolerance, and because in some cases there are already more effective medications available.

Evaluation of the hazards of marijuana is made difficult because of the emotionalism that clouds the issue. In the past, dangers were often highly exaggerated, equating the least use of marijuana with insanity and violent crime, as portrayed in the 1936 film *Reefer Madness*, which has become highly popular for its absurd view of marijuana's effects. Predictably, such hysteria and exaggeration created distrust and disbelief among marijuana users who found that the drug most often put them in a pleasant, relaxed, positive mood.

At the present time, little is known about the hazards of moderate marijuana use (less than once a week). Like alcohol, moderate indulgence seems to produce no apparent symptons. This should not be taken to mean that marijuana use is without risk, any more than the use of alcohol is without risk. In fact, there is much less known about the long-term effects of marijuana on human health and society than is known about the effects of alcohol. Although cannabis has been used for centuries, it is only since the mid-1960's that its use has become widespread, and scientific investigation of it thus is only in the beginning stages.

There are considerable research problems for those investigating marijuana. For example, the active principle of marijuana delta-9-tetrahydrocannabinol (THC), is only one of over four hundred chemicals known to be in the cannabis plant, and its chemical composition alters continuously as the plant grows and after it is harvested. Only recently has a federal marijuana farm in Mississippi been able to supply researchers with quality-controlled marijuana of known composition. In addition, because recent years have seen the introduction of marijuana with much higher levels of THC, some of the earlier research using marijuana with lower levels is no longer relevant.

It is not surprising that scientific studies have

produced conflicting evidence on the health risks of marijuana. The issue is still so controversial that a dispassionate attitude is very difficult to maintain. On the one hand, marijuana advocates make an obvious point: today millions of people smoke marijuana without exhibiting brain damage or increased illness due to a breakdown in the immune system. And such advocates have no trouble quoting studies that show marijuana is safe. On the other hand, critics of marijuana point out that there are far too many "burnouts" and dropouts among heavy users to discount the research that shows marijuana to be a risk, and they remind skeptics that it took fifty years of research to establish a scientific link between cigarette smoking and cancer. Extreme positions on either side of the issue are unhelpful. We prefer a commonsense approach to the problem—namely, that regular or occasional smoking of a substance that contains some four hundred chemicals of uncertain toxicity is likely to produce some adverse effects, even if only temporarily. As we have said, taking drugs is taking risks.

An additional reason often given for advising caution is that marijuana use is illegal. In reality, however, nowadays there is very little enforcement of the laws against possession of small amounts of marijuana for personal use. The movement to decriminalize marijuana has led eleven states to reduce penalities for possession of such amounts to a petty misdemeanor (a small fine and no jail time), although under federal law and most state laws, possession is still a misdemeanor (a first offense under federal law is punishable by up to a five-thousand-dollar fine and a year in jail). Sale of marijuana is a more serious offense under both state and federal laws.

Although decriminalization is a humane attempt to adjust the law to the reality of widespread marijuana use, many observers have noted the inherent contradiction that is involved in easing penalties for users while maintaining penalties for suppliers: demand for marijuana has predictably increased, making suppliers richer and more willing to take risks. And the risks in turn diminish because, as the number of suppliers increases, a greater number of them are able to evade arrest by overextended law-enforcement agencies.

DRUGS WITH MULTIPLE EFFECTS ON THE CENTRAL NERVOUS SYSTEM

DRUG TYPE: PHENCYCLIDINE (PCP, ANGEL DUST)

Phencyclidine is a complex chemical whose shorthand name, PCP, is derived from its scientific designation, 1-(1-phenylcyclohexyl)piperdine hydrochloride. PCP was developed in the 1950's by Parke, Davis and Company under the trade name Sernyl for use as a surgical anesthetic. Although it proved effective for this purpose, producing anesthesia without depressing vital functions, it had such adverse side effects (severe disorientation, hallucinations, manic behavior) that its use was discontinued in 1965. However, it was judged to be an effective anesthetic for nonhuman primates and other large animals, and since 1967 phencyclidine has been approved for veterinary use under the trade name Sernylan. Phencyclidine has also been a focus of research in psychiatric medicine because it mimics both low-level brain damage and the primary symptoms of schizophrenia.

Although it is a pharmacologically complex drug, phencyclidine is easy to synthesize; it can be produced from a few readily available and inexpensive chemicals using simple equipment in basement or mobile laboratories. But most PCP is now manufactured in

167

larger, well-equipped laboratories capable of producing very large quantities with a street value of millions of dollars. PCP is sold in the form of pills, capsules, rock crystal, or liquid, but it is most frequently sold as a powder in a variety of colors and in doses of from one to ten milligrams.

PCP can be swallowed or injected, but the preferred methods of use are inhaling it up the nostrils or smoking it sprinkled on a joint of parsley, mint, oregano, catnip, or low-grade marijuana. By snorting or smoking, the user has better control over the effects of the drug. Occasionally, cigarettes are dipped in liquid phencyclidine or, infrequently, PCP is administered by drops in the eye.

PCP first appeared as a street drug in the mid-sixties. Its use peaked between 1973 and 1975, when users discovered that smoking it provided better control. Since then its use has declined somewhat as PCP's adverse effects have become better known, but it is still a major part of the multiple drug user's repertoire. Originally sold in tablet form, it was marketed under such names as T-tabs, PeaCe Pills, and LBJ. It was also sold to the gullible as THC (the psychoactive agent in marijuana), and it is still known in some cities as "tic," "tish," or "titch." But the most common slang names are angel dust and hog.

Other street names for compounds that contain varying amounts of PCP include aurora borealis, busy bee, buzz, Cadillac, crystal, crystal flakes, cyclone, Detroit pink, dummy dust, dust, elephant, embalming fluid, erth, goon, green, green tea, horse tranks, killerjoint (KJ), killerweed (KW), kools, lovely, mintweed, mist, monkey dust, monkey tranquilizer, peace, peaceweed, rocket fuel, scuffle, sheets, shermans, snorts, soma, supergrass, superjoint, superweed, surfer, T, TAC, TIC, TT-1, wack-wack, wolf, zoom. Although these street names vary from region to region, they are not all synonymous but are used to differentiate various forms and strengths of PCP. Crystal, for example, is generally reserved for the purest form, which is white and crystalline; angel dust is considered to be good-quality PCP that is cut with corn sugar; rocket fuel is yellowish and considered an inferior grade; and killer weed generally means marijuana laced with PCP.

Effects

PCP is an extraordinary drug with a wide range of possible effects. It exhibits the properties of general and local anesthetics, psychomotor stimulants, sedatives, and hallucinogens, thus making it possible for the same user to have quite different experiences with the same dose on different occasions. PCP is most commonly used in a group setting, and the social rituals and expectations of the group greatly influence the drug's effects, as do the expectations of the user.

At present, exactly how phencyclidine affects the body is not clear, but when snorted or smoked, the effects begin immediately, peak in thirty to ninety minutes, and last up to six hours or longer, depending on the dose. Physiological effects include high blood pressure, increased pulse rate, rapid eye movements (nystagmus), sweating, flushing, dizziness, difficulty in controlling body movements (ataxia), and occasional episodes of nausea and vomiting.

Low doses generally produce a mild euphoria and stimulation (sometimes called a buzz), increased talkativeness and sociability, and a feeling of alertness and strength, with occasional bursts of energy. Some users report that their motivation was increased, and physical tasks such as light housework, lawn mowing, or athletics became easier.

Moderate to high doses, being "stoned" or

169

"wasted," produce a body-wide anesthesia in which coordination is difficult and speech slurred. A "numbed-out" feeling is often described, particularly in the legs and feet, so that walking can be an amusing experience, like walking on marshmallows or clouds. An insensitivity to pain and touch and diminished aural and visual perception are also part of this anesthetic effect. Body-image distortions, out-of-body experiences, and time distortions are often reported: arms and legs can seem very long or very small or disjointed; parts of the body can feel like they are melting; odd sensations of being able to observe oneself from somewhere else are sometimes experienced. At present these effects are attributed to the drug's blockage of proprioceptive feedback mechanisms—that is, an inability to sense internal bodily conditions. This overall effect is considered "spacey"; time is slowed down, but the mind seems to be speeded up or "wired." Users report that the world seems quite different and that they feel like they are floating. Although speech, coordination, and thought appear disordered, internal awareness seems intense. As one user put it, "My body wasn't up to doin' nothin', but my brain was just cruisin' along!"

The importance of proprioceptive feedback blockage and environment on the subjective effects of PCP has been confirmed by sensory-deprivation experiments that showed PCP's effects were greatly diminished or nonexistent in a stimulus-free environment. PCP also intensifies moods, which can swing from high euphoria to severe depression. One striking effect of PCP is the frequency with which thoughts of death or deathly images occur, and many users find this to be a strangely pleasant experience and part of their fascination with PCP.

Still higher doses of phencyclidine (being

"zoned" or "ozoned") produce loss of muscular control, rigidity, stupor, and a blank or frozen stare. These physiological effects are frequently accompanied by hallucinations and dissociative reactions that include alternations in body image and body boundaries, a sense of unreality, feelings of isolation and profound loneliness, disorganized thinking, constant repetition of words or nonsense syllables, and a partial or complete loss of consciousness. Amnesia for the period of these episodes is frequently reported. Overdoses produce total unconsciousness, muscular rigidity, facial grimacing, and other severe effects of phencyclidine poisoning; and they are characteristically followed by a prolonged recovery period, which may last for weeks or months.

Risks

To date, very little information has been gathered on the long-term risks of PCP, but findings so far indicate that some tolerance appears to develop in chronic users, that there is no evidence of withdrawal symptoms or physical dependence, and that although some users describe a craving for the drug, psychological dependence is not commonly observed.

Recent studies of PCP users indicate that PCP is perceived as a powerful drug. However, contrary to the opinions of some drug experts and some recent media accounts, these studies report that users do not see uncontrollable violence as a risk. They are more concerned about overdosing and about becoming a burnout—someone whose mental functions have been impaired by chronic use of PCP. Prolonged use can cause memory disorders, general disorientation, speech difficulties, visual disturbances, personality change, emotional depression, anxiety, nervousness,

171

and suicidal tendencies. These conditions improve when PCP use is discontinued, although they can persist for days and weeks and sometimes up to a year, in daily high-dose users. There is also some preliminary evidence that PCP can damage brain tissue.

Overdoses result in acute phencyclidine poisoning in which a coma, often lengthy, is followed by disorientation, confusion, delirium, prolonged irritability and depression, and emotional fluctuations—all of which can necessitate psychiatric care. Occasionally an acute state of psychosis persists manifested by paranoia and aggressive behavior or by severe depression and suicidal thoughts, which requires extensive psychiatric hospitalization.

Accidental and suicidal deaths from high doses of phencyclidine have been reported, and respiratory failure is sometimes the suspected cause. The mental confusion and incoordination caused by PCP renders users incapable of responding to dangerous situations, and injury and death have resulted from burning, falling from high places, drowning, driving accidents, and violent outbursts. PCP is thus said to have a *behavioral toxicity*.

PCP poses additional risks to users when it is adulturated or misrepresented. Analyzed street samples have contained anywhere from ten percent to one hundred percent PCP. Because it is so cheap and easy to manufacture, PCP is very frequently misrepresented as THC, LSD, or some other hallucinogen; and as a general rule any street drug with a bizarre name will contain some PCP. It has been identified as part of compounds that are sold as amphetamine, belladonna, cocaine, cannabinol, DMT, hashish, marijuana, MDA, mescaline, PCPA, peyote, psilocybin, and STP.

In short, PCP users seriously risk anesthesia, impaired mental functioning, paranoia and other psychiatric emergency reactions, acute behavioral toxicity that can result in death or injury, and burnout.

Remarks

The unpredictability and power of PCP are seen as a challenge by some, but others regard it as a "garbage drug." Users who like it are drawn to the idea of an unusual trip, and experienced users have learned to manage the possible adverse effects of the drug by testing the potency of the particular batch they are using, carefully measuring the dose and controlling the setting in which the drug is taken. Because they have positive expectations they are able to weather the sometimes-frightening distortions of time, space, body, and thought. Risk-taking is a strong motivation for PCP users, especially for adolescents who give high status to those who can control the effects of the drug.

PCP use currently appears to predominate among thirteen- to seventeen-year-olds, and this age-related usage is one of the best illustrations of the social nature of drug use. Older youths lose interest in PCP as they begin to think about jobs and their futures. PCP appeals to adolescents who are "looking for action" and who want to test the boundaries of their world by expanding their drug repertoires beyond beer and marijuana. Use of PCP becomes symbolic of membership and status within the peer group.

Users' expectations and the social and behavioral style of their peer group have a strong influence on the way PCP's effects are perceived. Some groups value the mental exploration of the hallucinogenic aspects of moderate doses of PCP, while others, usually rowdier in their public behavior, prefer to be "spaced out" on higher doses.

173

There is currently a public stereotype of PCP users as violent and irrational. Many users tend to be baffled by this perception because sophisticated techniques for using PCP have reduced the likelihood of adverse reactions, and any that do occur are usually managed by the group. However, there are numerous accounts linking PCP use to self-inflicted wounds, attacks on bystanders, unusual accidents under strange circumstances, and bizarre tales of superhuman strength and irrational outbursts of violence—all by individuals said to be under the influence of PCP. Investigations of such outbursts have indicated that they usually occur outside of a normal setting for drug use and often under the considerable stress of confrontation with police or emergency-room personnel.

Thus, under usual circumstances of PCP use, violence seems to be infrequent. This is not to say that violence does not occur, but rather that it does not inevitably occur as some exaggerated accounts have suggested. But aside from this issue of PCP-induced violence, the drug does have a potential for causing great harm to users. In recognition of the severe behavioral toxicity of phencyclidine, the U.S. Congress in 1978 imposed penalities for its manufacture and distribution that are harsher than those for any other nonnarcotic violation of the Controlled Substances Act.

Footnotes

[1] Bernard Gavzer, *Parade*, November 22, 1981, p. 21.

AFTERWORD

As this book was going to press, it was evident that there is continuing national concern, from the White House to the schoolhouse, about the pervasiveness of drug use. The awareness is growing that drug use has serious consequences both for the individual and for society. Children are particularly vulnerable, and drug use by children creates a difficult problem that defies simple solutions.

The information and ideas contained in these pages have been presented as a guide, not as a cure-all. Throughout the writing, we have been aware not only of the complex nature of drug use, but of the emotional responses that often interfere with calm and intelligent discussion of the subject. Our aim has been to be as clear and objective as possible.

We believe that parents can—and must—make a determined effort to help their children confront the dangerous consequences of drug use. It is our hope that KIDS & DRUGS: A PARENT'S GUIDE has provided parents—and children—with information, effective activities, and inspiration to stem drug use. The energy and talents of our young people are resources too valuable to be wasted on drugs.

INDEX